# The
# Wit & Wisdom
# of London

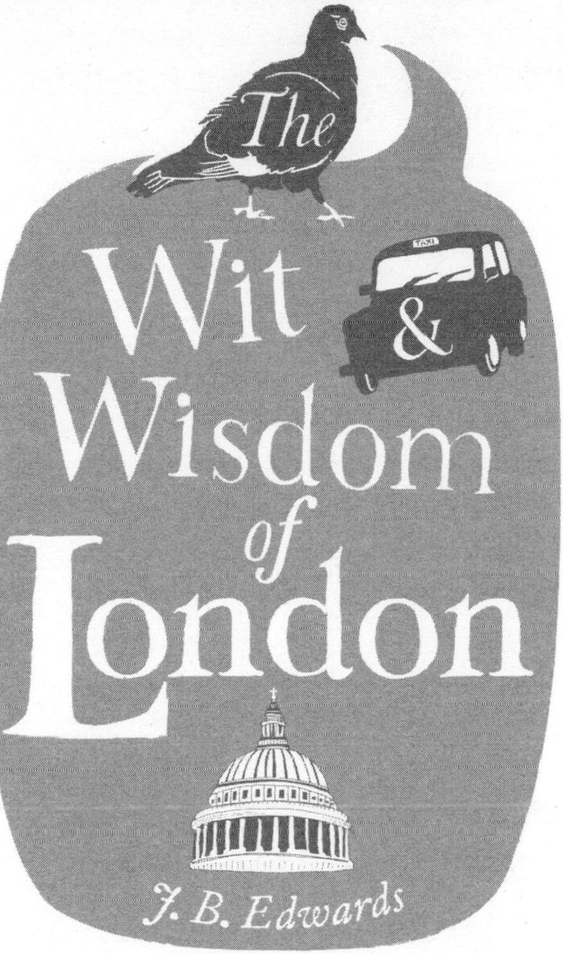

# The Wit & Wisdom of London

## J. B. Edwards

Illustrated by Lucy Stephens

10 9 8 7 6 5 4 3 2 1

First published in 2012 by Virgin Books, an imprint of Ebury Publishing
A Random House Group Company

Copyright © J B Edwards 2012

The author has asserted his right under the Copyright, Designs and Patents
Act 1988 to be identified as the author of this work.

Copyright © in the individual quotations as identified in the book

Illustrations by Lucy Stephens

Every reasonable effort has been made to contact copyright holders of
material reproduced in this book. If any have inadvertently been overlooked,
the publishers would be glad to hear from them and make good in future
editions any errors or omissions brought to their attention.

www.randomhouse.co.uk

Addresses for companies within The Random House Group Limited can be
found at www.randomhouse.co.uk/offices.htm

The Random House Group Limited Reg. No. 954009

A CIP catalogue record for this book is available from the British Library

The Random House Group Limited supports The Forest Stewardship
Council (FSC®), the leading international forest certification organisation.
Our books carrying the FSC label are printed on FSC® certified paper. FSC
is the only forest certification scheme endorsed by the leading environmental
organisations, including Greenpeace. Our paper procurement policy can be
found at www.randomhouse.co.uk/environment

Designed by K DESIGN, Somerset
Printed and bound by CPI Group (UK) Ltd, Croydon, CR0 4YY

ISBN: 9780753540930

To buy books by your favourite authors and register for offers, visit
www.randomhouse.co.uk

# Contents

# Introduction

Londoners are lucky to be surrounded by so many visible reminders of the city's long history. Compared to the modern metropolises of the USA or the glittering mega cities of Japan and China, London can seem almost impossibly ancient and quaint. The landmarks of the city centre are familiar the world over, and cherished by the millions of tourists and native Londoners who visit them each year.

But the long centuries of London's growth and its present geographical sprawl mean that even in the most unprepossessing parts of town, there are many noteworthy traces of the past. Within a fifteen-minute walk of my house in south London – an area that was mostly countryside until the start of the twentieth century – I pass a former Dissenters' Chapel that Daniel Defoe attended, the London home of Thomas Hardy, and a common listed in the Domesday Book.

But while the physical reminders of London's past are there for anyone to visit, the voices of its former residents – who are responsible for the city we know and love – are harder to find. In this book, I've aimed to collect the best of what's been said about London through the ages, so we can appreciate the great city we have inherited, and have a better understanding of what it meant to those who came before us.

Many of the feelings expressed in these pages will be instantly familiar to modern visitors. From Mark Twain's complaints about his decrepit hotel to a twelfth-century monk's concern over 'the immoderate drinking of foolish persons', it is somehow comforting to realise we are not alone in suffering the occasional annoyances that London forces upon us.

Other problems have thankfully not persisted into the present age. The Thames is no longer the 'Stygian pool reeking with ineffable and unbearable horror' that Disraeli spoke of in the nineteenth century, and it's quite a few years since we needed to be wary about having our wigs stolen from our heads in the street, as playwright John Gay was in the 1710s.

Throughout London's history, residents and visitors have spoken most of all about the city itself: its vastness and intensity and the special feeling that comes from being caught up in the unending busyness of the streets. The quotes in this book capture the delights as well as the horrors of the city: on the one hand, the wealth and the promise of a better tomorrow for the lucky few; on the other, its poverty and the uncaring face it shows to those who fail to make the grade. I've tried to show a complicated place from every angle, in the words of those who saw it at its worst and at its best through the centuries.

London will speak to you in all its variety in the pages that follow, and I hope that the next time you are out enjoying the sights of the city, you will also hear its voice.

J B Edwards, Tooting, London

# London
# Defined

ALTHOUGH LONDON MAY seem too vast and contradictory ever to allow itself to be summarised in a few words, or a few thousand, many commentators have written epigrams that manage to capture aspects of the truth of the metropolis.

'London goes beyond any boundary or convention. It contains every wish or word ever spoken, every action or gesture ever made, every harsh or noble statement ever expressed. It is illimitable. It is Infinite London.'

PETER ACKROYD, novelist and historian,
*London: The Biography*, 2000

'London is a bad habit one hates to lose.'

ANONYMOUS popular saying, twentieth century

'London is the epitome of our times, and the Rome of today.'

RALPH WALDO EMERSON, American poet,
*English Traits*, 1856

'Never was there a dingier, uglier, less picturesque city than London … it is really wonderful that so much brick and stone, for centuries together, should have been built up with so poor a result.'

NATHANIEL HAWTHORNE, American novelist,
*English Notebooks*, 1853

'The Devil's drawing room.'

LORD BYRON, poet, *Don Juan*, 1821

'London: a nation, not a city.'

BENJAMIN DISRAELI, politician and novelist, *Lothair*, 1870

'Uniquely among transport systems, London Underground typifies the city itself.'

CHRISTIAN WOLMAR, writer and transport commentator,
*The Subterranean Railway*, 2004

'A flat black bug, that is London.'

PAUL VERLAINE, French poet, 1872

'London, that great cesspool into which all the loungers and idlers of the Empire are irresistibly drained.'

SIR ARTHUR CONAN DOYLE, writer,
*A Study in Scarlet*, 1887

'It is difficult to speak adequately or justly of London. It is not a pleasant place; it is not agreeable, or cheerful, or easy, or exempt from reproach. It is only magnificent.'

HENRY JAMES, American novelist,
*The Notebooks of Henry James*, 1881

'London is the clearing-house of the world.'

JOSEPH CHAMBERLAIN, politician, 1836–1914

'London is only a huge shop, with a hotel on the upper storeys.'

GEORGE GISSING, novelist, *New Grub Street*, 1891

'I remember London as a city of gardens where the birds woke me every morning.'

ALBERT CAMUS, French author and philosopher, 1913–1960

'London is a roost for every bird.'

BENJAMIN DISRAELI, politician and novelist, 1804–1881

# Destination London

LONDON DOES NOT only fire the imagination of those already living there. It also shines like a beacon in the dreams of countless people who one day hope to see it, to enter its infinite boundaries – and finally to become a part of it themselves.

'When we came upon Highgate Hill and had a view of London, I was all life and joy. I repeated Cato's soliloquy on the immortality of the soul, and my soul bounded forth to a certain prospect of happy futurity. I sung all manner of songs, and began to make one about an amorous meeting with a pretty girl, the burthen of which was as follows:

> She gave me *this*, I gave her *that*;
> And tell me, had she not tit for tat?

I gave three huzzas, and we went briskly in.'

JAMES BOSWELL, diarist, on returning to London, 1762

'London conquers most who enter it.'

THOMAS DE QUINCEY, author, 1800

'A country gentleman should bring his lady to visit London as soon as he can, that they may have agreeable topicks for conversation when they are by themselves.'

SAMUEL JOHNSON, writer and polymath, 1709–1784

"'I am going to London," said Dorothea.
"How can you always live in a street? And you will be
so poor.'"

GEORGE ELIOT, novelist, *Middlemarch*, 1872

'The night was dark and stormy,
But blithe of heart were they,
For shining in the distance
The lights of London lay.
O gleaming lights of London, that gem of the city's crown;
What fortunes be within you, O Lights of London Town!'

GEORGE R SIMS, writer, song from *Lights o' London*, 1881

'As I came down the Highgate Hill
I met the sun's bravado,
And saw below me, fold on fold,
Grey to pearl and pearl to gold,
This London like a land of old,
The land of Eldorado.'

HENRY HOWARTH BASHFORD, poet, *Romances*, 1917

'We may say that London begins where tree trunks commence to be black.'

FORD MADOX FORD, novelist, 1905

'London loomed up before me, wonderful, mystical as Assyrian Babylon, as full of unheard-of-things and great unveilings.'

ARTHUR MACHEN, novelist and mystic, 1863–1947

'A mighty mass of brick, and smoke, and shipping,
Dirty and dusty, but as wide as eye
Could reach, with here and there a sail just skipping
In sight, then lost amidst the forestry
Of masts; a wilderness of steeples peeping
On tiptoe through their sea-coal canopy;
A huge, dun cupola, like a foolscap crown
On a fool's head – and there is London Town.'

LORD BYRON, poet, *Don Juan*, 1821

'London is where people go in order to come back from it sadder and wiser.'

MARTIN AMIS, novelist, *The Rachel Papers*, 1973

'Forget the six counties overhung with smoke,
Forget the snorting steam and piston stroke,
Forget the spreading of the hideous town;
Think rather of the pack-horse on the down,
And dream of London, small and white and clean,
The clear Thames bordered by its gardens green.'

WILLIAM MORRIS, poet, *The Earthly Paradise*, 1870

# London History

THE TWO THOUSAND years of London are not easily reduced into bite-sized morsels, but the quotes gathered here give a flavour of the city at key times in its history, from the earliest confrontations between the native Britons and the Roman invaders, to the perilous nights of the Blitz in the last century.

# Roman London

'Caesar … leads his army into the territories of Cassivellaunus to the river Thames; which river can be forded in one place only, and that with difficulty. When he had arrived there, he perceived that numerous forces of the enemy were marshalled on the other bank of the river; the bank also was defended by sharp stakes fixed in front, and stakes of the same kind fixed under the water were covered by the river.'

JULIUS CAESAR'S invading army confront the tribal chief Cassivellaunus on the banks of the Thames, from *'Commentarii De Bello Gallico'*, *c.* 40 BC

'Suetonius … marched amidst a hostile population to Londinium, which, though undistinguished by the name of a colony, was much frequented by a number of merchants and trading vessels …

'Unmoved by lamentations and appeals, Suetonius gave the signal for departure. The inhabitants were allowed to accompany him. But those who stayed because they were women, or old, or attached to the place, were slaughtered by the enemy … About seventy thousand citizens and allies, it appeared, fell … For it was not on making prisoners and selling them, or on any of the barter of war, that the enemy was bent, but on slaughter, on the gibbet, the fire and the cross, like men soon about to pay the penalty, and meanwhile snatching at instant vengeance.'

Account of the destruction of London by QUEEN BOUDICA and the
Iceni, from *The Annals of Tacitus*, AD 60 or 61

'Primus has made ten tiles. Enough! … Austalis has been taking off on his own every day for the last fortnight … for shame! … London, next door to the temple of Isis … Clementinus fashioned this tile.'

These are the earliest known words of a Londoner, scratched upon
pieces of tile, first century AD

# Medieval London

'Lundenwic … on the banks of the Thames … a trading centre for many nations that visit it by land and sea.'

The venerable BEDE, monk, AD 731

'All the beauty of this island is confined to London; which, although sixty miles distant to the sea, possesses all the advantages to be desired in a maritime town; being situated on the river Thames, which is very much affected by the tide … and London is so much benefited by this ebb and flow of the river, that vessels of 100 tons burden can come up to the city, and ships of any size to within five miles of it.'

ANDREAS TREVISAN, Venetian diplomat, 1498

'I would sell London if I could find a buyer.'

Attributed to KING RICHARD I, monarch, 1157–1199

'Amid the noble cities of the world, the City of London, throne of the English kingdom, is one which has spread its fame far and wide, its wealth and merchandise to great distances, raised its head on high. It is blessed by a wholesome climate, blessed too in Christ's religion, in the strength of its fortifications, in the nature of its site, the repute of its citizens, the honour of its matrons; happy in its sports, prolific in noble men.'

WILLIAM FITZSTEPHEN, monk, *c.* 1180

## The Gunpowder Plot, 1605

'I would advise you, as you tender your life, to devise some excuse to shift of your attendance of this Parliament, for God and man hath concurred to punish the wickedness of this time … For though there be no appearance of any stir, yet I say they shall receive a terrible blow, the Parliament, and yet they shall not see who hurts them.'

Author unconfirmed, letter to LORD MONTEAGLE warning him of the Gunpowder Plot, 26 October 1605

'Remember, remember the fifth of November,
gunpowder, treason and plot,
I see no reason why gunpowder treason
should ever be forgot.
Guy Fawkes, Guy Fawkes, 'twas his intent
to blow up the King and the Parliament.
Three score barrels of powder below,
Poor old England to overthrow:
By God's providence he was catch'd
With a dark lantern and burning match.
Holloa boys, holloa boys, make the bells ring.
Holloa boys, holloa boys, God save the King!'

Traditional rhyme commemorating the plot to blow up the Houses of
Parliament, as reproduced from the Tower of London archive,
seventeenth century

# The Restoration of Charles II, 1660

'29th. This day his Majesty Charles the Second came to London after a sad and long exile and calamitous suffering both of the King and Church, being seventeen years. This was also his birthday, and with a triumph of above 20,000 horse and foot, brandishing their swords and shouting with inexpressible joy; the ways strewed with flowers, the bells ringing, the streets hung with tapissry, fountains running with wine; the Mayor, Aldermen, and all the companies in their liveries, chains of gold, and banners; Lords and Nobles clad in cloth of silver, gold, and velvet; the windows and balconies all set with ladies; trumpets, music, and myriads of people flocking, even so far as from Rochester, so as they were seven hours in passing the city, even from two in the afternoon to nine at night.

'I stood in the Strand and beheld it, and blessed God. And all this was done without one drop of blood shed, and by that very army which rebelled against him; but it was the Lord's doing, for such a restoration was never mentioned in any history ancient or modern, since the return of the Jews from the Babylonish captivity; nor so joyful a day and so bright ever seen in this nation, this happening when to expert or effect it was past all human policy.'

JOHN EVELYN, diarist, on the Restoration of Charles II,
29 May 1660

# The Great Plague, 1665

'I went away and walked to Greenwich, on my way seeing a coffin with a dead body therein, dead of the plague, lying in an open close belonging to Coome farm, which was carried out last night and the parish hath not appointed anybody to bury it – but only set a watch there day and night, that nobody should go thither or come hence, which is a most cruel thing – this disease making us more cruel to one another than we are to dogs.'

SAMUEL PEPYS, diarist, 22 August 1665

'As the desolation was greater during those terrible times, so the amazement of the people increased, and a thousand unaccountable things they would do in the violence of their fright, as others did the same in the agonies of their distemper, and this part was very affecting.

'Some went roaring and crying and wringing their hands along the street; some would go praying and lifting up their hands to heaven, calling upon God for mercy. I cannot say, indeed, whether this was not in their distraction, but, be it so, it was still an indication of a more serious mind, when they had the use of their senses, and was much better, even as it was, than the frightful yellings and cryings that every day, and especially in the evenings, were heard in some streets.'

DANIEL DEFOE, novelist, A *Journal of the Plague Year*, 1722

'There was still a question among the learned … and that was in what manner to purge the house and goods where the plague had been, and how to render them habitable again, which had been left empty during the time of the plague.

'Abundance of perfumes and preparations were described by the physicians, some of one kind and some of another, in which the people who listened to them put themselves to a great, and indeed, in my opinion, to an unnecessary expense; and the poorer people, who only set open their windows night and day, burned brimstone, pitch, and gunpowder, and such things in their rooms, did as well as the best.'

DANIEL DEFOE, novelist, *A Journal of the Plague Year*, 1722

## The Great Fire of London, 1666

*The Great Fire of London changed the city forever. The blaze began at Thomas Farriner's bakery on Pudding Lane on Sunday 2 September 1666 and soon raged out of control. Over three terrible days and nights, it destroyed over 13,000 mostly wooden buildings in London's densely populated centre, as well as the medieval St Paul's Cathedral. These eyewitness accounts by the diarist John Evelyn convey the horror and devastation of the fire.*

'The conflagration was so universal, and the people so astonished, that from the beginning, I know not by what despondency or fate, they hardly stirred to quench it, so that there was nothing seen or heard but crying out and lamentation, running about like distracted creatures without at all attempting to save their goods.'

'3rd. The fire continuing, after dinner I took my coach with my wife and son and went to the Bank side in Southwark, where we beheld that dismal spectacle, the whole city in dreadful flames near the water side; all the houses from the Bridge, all Thames-street, and upwards towards Cheapside, down to the Three Cranes, were now consumed: and so returned exceeding astonished what would come of the rest.'

'Oh the miserable and calamitous spectacle! such as haply the world has not seen since the foundation of it, nor be outdone till the universal conflagration thereof. All the sky was a fiery aspect, like the top of a burning oven, and the light seen above 40 miles round about for many nights.

'God grant mine eyes may never behold the like, who now saw above 10,000 houses all in one flame; the noise and cracking and thunder of the impetuous flames, the shrieking of women and children, the hurry of people,

the fall of towers, houses and churches, was like a hideous
storm, and the air all about so hot and inflamed that at the
last one was not able to approach it, so that they were
forced to stand still and let the flames burn on, which they
did for near two miles in length and on in breadth. The
clouds also of smoke were dismal and reached upon
computation near 50 miles in length.'

*On 7 September 1666, two days after the Great Fire had
been brought under control, Evelyn took a walk through
the devastated city.*

'7th. I went out this morning on foot from White-hall as
far as London Bridge, through the late Fleet-street,
Ludgate hill, by St Paul's, Cheapside, Exchange,
Bishopsgate, Aldersgate, and out to Moorfields, thence
through Cornhill, &c. with extraordinary difficulty,
clambering over heaps of yet smoking rubbish, and
frequently mistaking where I was. The ground under
my feet so hot, that it even burnt the soles of my shoes.

'In five or six miles of traversing about, I did not see
one load of timber unconsumed, nor many stones but
what were calcined white as snow. The people who now
walked about the ruins appeared like men in some dismal
desert, or rather in some great city laid waste by a cruel

enemy; to which was added the stench that came from some poor creatures' bodies, beds and other combustible goods.'

'I then went towards Islington and Highgate, whence one might have seen some 200,000 people of all ranks and degrees dispersed and lying along by their heaps of what they could save from the fire, deploring their loss, and though ready to perish for hunger and destitution, yet not asking one penny for relief, which to me appeared a stranger sight than any I had yet beheld.'

'10th. I went again to the ruins, for it was no longer a city.'

## The Gordon Riots, 1780

'Akerman [Keeper of Newgate Prison] had in his custody four prisoners, taken in the riot; these the mob went to his house and demanded … By eight o'clock, Akerman's house was in flames. I went close to it, and never saw anything so dreadful. The prison was, as I said, a remarkably strong building; but, determined to force it, they broke the gates with crows and other instruments, and climbed up the outside of the cell part, which joins the two great wings of the building, where the felons were confined; and I stood where I plainly saw their operations. They broke the roof, tore away the rafters, and having got ladders they descended. Not Orpheus himself had more courage or better luck; flames all around them, and a body of soldiers expected, they defied and laughed at all opposition.'

GEORGE CRABBE, poet and diarist, records the destruction of Newgate Prison during the anti-Catholic Gordon Riots, June 1780

## Queen Victoria's Diamond Jubilee, 1897

'No one ever, I believe, has met with such an ovation as was given to me, passing through those six miles of streets … The crowds were quite indescribable and their enthusiasm truly marvellous and deeply touching. The cheering was quite deafening and every face seemed to be filled with (real) joy.'

QUEEN VICTORIA on her Diamond Jubilee procession, which travelled from St Paul's Cathedral, across London Bridge, through south London and back past Parliament to Buckingham Palace, in her journal, 22 June 1897

'For in Her Majesty, as she sat in her magnificent carriage, amid all the splendour of her court, the glistening of gold, the shining of sabres and the pomp of cavalry, in her quiet simple dress, all of us recognised a grand example of humility, of patience, of long suffering – in a word, womanliness.'

*Vanity Fair* on Queen Victoria, 24 June 1897

## The London Olympics, 1908

'News of the start [of the marathon race] at Windsor came to swarms of Londoners as they took their way to Paddington and Baker-street Stations to catch the race on the outskirts. The Prince of Wales had fired the electric gun ... All the places on the route where the train touched were buzzing with people. The City must have been half empty, the City man and his clerk were here in their tens of thousands.'

*The Guardian*, on the marathon race of the first Olympic Games ever held in London, 25 July 1908

'It would be no exaggeration to say that the finish of the marathon at the 1908 Olympics in London was the most thrilling athletic event that has occurred since that Marathon race in ancient Greece, where the victor fell at the goal and, with a wave of triumph, died.'

*The New York Times*, 25 July 1908

## London in the Second World War

*London Can Take It!*

Defiant title of a short film about the Blitz, 1940

'It is not the walls that make the city, but the people who live within them. The walls of London may be battered, but the spirit of the Londoner stands resolute and undismayed.'

GEORGE VI, British monarch, broadcast to the Empire during German bomber offensive, 23 September 1940

'Little does [Hitler] know the spirit of the British nation, or the tough fibre of the Londoners.'

SIR WINSTON CHURCHILL, Prime Minister, 11 September 1940

'Everyone was absolutely determined, secretly delighted with the privilege of holding up Hitler.'

HUMPHREY JENNINGS, documentary film-maker, 1940

'Doctor Paul Joseph Goebbels said recently that the nightly air raids have had a terrific effect on the morale of the people of London. The good doctor is absolutely right. Today the morale of the people is higher than ever before. They are fused together, not by fear, but by a surging spirit of courage the like of which the world has never known. They know that thousands of them will die. But they would rather stand up and face death than kneel down and face the kind of existence the conqueror would impose upon them.'

QUENTIN REYNOLDS, war correspondent, 1940

'The vast mass of London itself, fought street by street, could easily devour an entire hostile army, and we would rather see London laid in ashes and ruins than that it should be tamely and abjectly enslaved.'

SIR WINSTON CHURCHILL, Prime Minister, 14 July 1940

'I'm glad we've been bombed. It makes me feel I can look the East End in the face.'

QUEEN ELIZABETH, the future Queen Mother, after bombing damaged Buckingham Palace, September 1940

'It was as impersonal as the plague, as though the city were infested with enormous verminous insects.'

EVELYN WAUGH, novelist, describing the V1 attacks of 1944

## London Today

'The London Games will be designed for the athletes and we will provide them with the very best venues and the very best conditions to pursue their sporting dreams in London.'

LORD SEBASTIAN COE, Chairman of the London 2012 Organising Committee, 2005

'Finally, I wish to speak directly to those who came to London today to take life. I know that you personally do not fear giving up your own life in order to take others – that is why you are so dangerous. But I know you fear that you may fail in your long-term objective to destroy our free society and I can show you why you will fail.

'In the days that follow, look at our airports, look at our sea ports and look at our railway stations and, even after your cowardly attack, you will see that people from the rest of Britain, people from around the world, will arrive in London to become Londoners and to fulfil their dreams and achieve their potential. They choose to come to London, as so many have come before, because they come to be free, they come to live the life they choose, they come to be able to be themselves.

'They flee you because you tell them how they should live. They don't want that and nothing you do, however many of us you kill, will stop that flight to our city where freedom is strong and where people can live in harmony with one another. Whatever you do, however many you kill, you will fail.'

KEN LIVINGSTONE, Mayor of London, speech in response to the London terrorist attacks, 7 July 2005

# London Transport

GETTING AROUND LONDON has long seemed to be one of the main obstacles facing its citizens, and complaints about the quality of the services, the surliness of fellow travellers, and the general *fullness* of London's transport network have been familiar down the centuries. Nevertheless, many have also found magic while travelling round the capital.

'The Gondola of London.'

BENJAMIN DISRAELI, politician and novelist, describing the
hansom cab, *Lothair*, 1870

'Art has to move you and design does not, unless it's a good
design for a bus.'

DAVID HOCKNEY, artist, 1988

'London, moreover, is rendered habitable by Hansom
cabs. Young Walshingham was a natural cab-taker; he was
an all-round, large-minded young man, and he had in the
course of their two days' stay taken Kipps into no less than
nine, so that Kipps was singularly not afraid of those
vehicles. He knew that wherever you were, so soon as you
were thoroughly lost, you said "Hi!" to a cab, and then
"Royal Grand Hotel."

Day and night these trusty conveyances are
returning the strayed Londoner back to his point of
departure, and were it not for their activity, in a little
while the whole population, so vast and incomprehensible
is the intricate complexity of this great city, would be
hopelessly lost for ever.'

H G WELLS, author, *Kipps*, 1905

'When he got into Fleet-street, there was "a stoppage", in which people in vehicles have the satisfaction of remaining stationary for half an hour, and envying the slowest pedestrians; and where policemen rush about, and seize hold of horses' bridles, and back them into shop-windows, by way of clearing the road and preventing confusion.'

CHARLES DICKENS, novelist, *Sketches by Boz*, 1836

'London externally has changed very much ... The traffic – it appears to me – has been increased still ... You see one street filled with carriages and buses and one or two horses, poor beasts feeling quite lonely in the crowded street. The smell is terrible; they say it is healthier than the smell of horses but quite sure it is not very pleasant.

'What may not be very healthy is to be injured by a motor-car or motor-bus ... The Londoners – like always – grumble about such a state of things but they are so many, you know, that they think it is better to improve the lives of several millions of living persons rather than to save the life of a few hundreds ...

'At Charing Cross we saw a motor-bus going to Lewisham and we took our seats at the top of it. It is something like the crossing of the channel when there are moderate breezes. I was almost seasick.'

ITALO SVEVO, Italian writer, 1908

'What is this that roareth thus?
Can it be a Motor Bus?
Yes, the smell and hideous hum
Indicat Motorem Bum!...
How shall wretches live like us
Cincti Bis Motoribus?
Domine, defende nos
Contra hos Motores Bos!'

A D GODLEY, English classicist, 'The Motor Bus', 1914

'I have known a man, dying a long way from London, sigh queerly for a sight of the gush of smoke that, on a platform of the Underground, one may see, escaping, in great woolly clots up a circular opening, by a grimy, rusted, iron shield, into the dim upper light.'

FORD MADOX FORD, novelist, *The Soul of London*, 1904

'The traffic of London used to roar with the mystery of man's adventure on the seas of life, like a vast seashell, murmuring a thrilling half-comprehensible story. Now it booms like monotonous, far-off guns, in a monotony of crushing something, crushing the earth, crushing out life, crushing everything dead.'

D H LAWRENCE, novelist,
'Why I Don't Like Living in London', 1928

'I fell in love with the Underground at an early age. It represented freedom and adventure, a seemingly limitless network of stations with wonderfully exotic names such as Cockfosters and Burnt Oak. There were no automatic gates in those days and for a couple of pence thrust into the hands of a ticket collector together with a mumbled mention of the previous station, I had the freedom of the system for the day.'

CHRISTIAN WOLMAR, writer and transport commentator,
*The Subterranean Railway*, 2004

'Although this curious and unique Metropolitan Railway has been termed underground, or subterranean, for nearly half its length it is open to the light and air of heaven, and where it does pass for various lengths beneath the surface, it is so well lighted and ventilated that the tunnels, instead of being close, dark, damp and offensive, are wide, spacious, clean and luminous, and more like a well-kept street at night, than a subterranean passage through the heart of the metropolis.'

*Illustrated London News*, on the opening of the first underground railway, 1862

'The road [track] now began to be uphill, and at the same time the air grew more foul. From King's Cross to Edgware Road, the ventilation is defective and the atmosphere more on a par with the "tween decks, forrud" of a modern ironclad in bad weather and that is saying a great deal. By the time we reached Gower Street I was coughing and spluttering like a boy with his first cigar.

'"It is a little unpleasant when you ain't used to it," said the driver, with the composure born of long usage, "but you ought to come on a hot summer day to get the real thing!"'

FRED JANE, journalist, 'Round the Underground on an Engine', *English Illustrated Magazine*, 1893

'Take the two-penny Tube and avoid all anxiety.'

Central London railway advertising slogan, 1905

'Why do all clerks and navvies in the railway trains look so sad and tired, so very sad and tired? I will tell you. It is because they know that the train is going right. It is because they know that whatever place they have taken a ticket for, that place they will reach. It is because after they have passed Sloane Square they know that the next station must be Victoria, and nothing but Victoria. Oh, their wild rapture! Oh, their eyes like stars and their souls again in Eden, if the next station were unaccountably Baker Street!'

G K CHESTERTON, novelist, *The Man Who Was Thursday*, 1908

'We need to end the appalling tendency of the present Livingstone regime in City Hall to treat fare-dodging as a kind of glorious Che Guevara two-fingers to the capitalist conspiracy.'

BORIS JOHNSON, politician, *Daily Telegraph*, 2008

'Beck's stroke of genius was to look at the problem of the map from the passengers' point of view, rather than in the way than those running the Underground perceived it. The map tidies up the chaos of the city, giving the impression the city is of a size and design that is comprehensible to both its inhabitants and visitors.'

CHRISTIAN WOLMAR, writer and transport commentator, on the creation of the London Underground map, *The Subterranean Railway*, 2004

'I was told the following at dinner last night. Two working men were in the Tube and began arguing over whether a certain peculiarly dressed person in the same carriage was or was not the Archbishop of Canterbury. They bet. To settle it, one of them went up to the person and said, "Please, sir, are you the Archbishop of Canterbury?"

'The reply was: "What the bloody hell has that got to do with you?"

'The workman went back to his mate and said: "No good, mate, the old cow won't give me a straight answer either way."'

ARNOLD BENNETT, novelist, diary entry, 13 December 1917

'London Underground took me on a tour of all the hidden places, the disused shafts and staircases … that was very interesting.'

RUTH RENDELL, novelist, b. 1930

'There is a paradox about the Underground. The miraculous system created by the pioneers is largely disliked and reviled by today's regular users.'

CHRISTIAN WOLMAR, writer and transport commentator, *The Subterranean Railway*, 2004

'Scars can come in useful. I have one myself above my left knee which is a perfect map of the London Underground.'

ALBUS DUMBLEDORE in *Harry Potter and the Philosopher's Stone* by J K Rowling, 1997

# London
# Landmarks

EVERYONE, WHETHER VISITOR or
resident Londoner, soon discovers their
favourite among London's countless historic
landmarks. Many of the city's former
inhabitants have been moved to celebrate,
and sometimes denigrate, the places that
stood out most in their experience of
London.

## The Tower of London

'Is not this house [the Tower of London] as nigh heaven as my own?'

SIR THOMAS MORE, humanist and statesman,
while imprisoned in the Tower, 1534

## St Paul's Cathedral

'Architecture aims at eternity.'

SIR CHRISTOPHER WREN, architect of
St Paul's Cathedral, 1632–1723

'St Paul's appeared to me unspeakably grand and noble, and the more so from the throng and bustle continually going on around its base, without in the least disturbing the sublime repose of its great dome, and, indeed, of all its massive height and breadth. Other edifices may crowd close to its foundation, and people may tramp as they like about it; but still the great cathedral is as quiet and serene as if it stood in the middle of Salisbury Plain.'

NATHANIEL HAWTHORNE, American novelist,
*English Notebooks*, 1854

'The first view of St Paul's, it may be supposed, overwhelmed us with awe; and I did not at that time imagine that the sense of magnitude could be more deeply impressed.

'One thing interrupted our pleasure. The superb objects of curiosity within the cathedral were shown for separate fees. There were seven, I think; and any one could be seen independently of the rest for a few pence. The whole amount was a trifle; fourteen pence, I think; but we were followed by a sort of persecution – "Would we not see the bell?" "Would we not see the model?" "Surely we would not go away without visiting the whispering gallery?" – solicitations which troubled the silence and sanctity of the place, and must tease others as it then teased us, who wished to contemplate in quiet this great monument of the national grandeur, which was at that very time beginning to take a station also in the land, as a depository for the dust of her heroes.'

THOMAS DE QUINCEY, writer, *Autobiographical Sketches*, 1853

## The City

'I have seen the West End, the parks, the fine squares; but I love the City far better. The City seems so much more in earnest; its business, its rush, its roar, are such serious things, sights, sounds ... At the West End you may be amused; but in the City you are deeply excited.'

CHARLOTTE BRONTË, novelist, 1849

'The shining buildings which now stand on the Roman wall contain brokers and dealers who are descendants ... of those who came to London in the first century. The City has always been established upon the imperatives of money and of trade.'

PETER ACKROYD, novelist and historian,
*London: The Biography*, 2000

'This part of London is a very Temple of Fame. Here rumours and gossip from all the regions of the world come pouring in, and from this echoing hall are reverberated back in strangely modified form echoes to all parts of Europe.'

CHARLES KNIGHT, author and editor, description of
Fleet Street from *London*, 1841

'There is no place in the town which I so much love to frequent as the Royal Exchange. It gives me a secret satisfaction, and in some measure gratifies my vanity, as I am an Englishman, to see so rich an assembly of countrymen and foreigners, consulting together upon the business of mankind, and making this metropolis a kind of emporium for the whole earth.'

JOSEPH ADDISON, journalist, *The Spectator*, 1711

'Take a view of the Royal Exchange in London, a place more venerable than many courts of justice, where the representatives of all nations meet for the benefit of mankind. There the Jew, the Mahometan, and the Christian transact together, as though they all professed the same religion, and give the name of infidel to none but bankrupts.'

VOLTAIRE, French philosopher, *Letters on England*, 1734

## The 'Gherkin'

'Deeply ugly.'

*Time Out Guide to London*, on 30 St Mary Axe, the 'Gherkin', 2003

'I rubbed my eyes and emitted a sigh as tragic as Prince Charles on beholding plans for the Gherkin.'

BORIS JOHNSON, Mayor of London,
*Daily Telegraph*, 2008

## The British Museum

'Yesterday I went out at about twelve, and visited the British Museum; an exceedingly tiresome affair. It quite crushes a person to see so much at once, and I wandered from hall to hall with a weary and heavy heart, wishing (Heaven forgive me!) that the Elgin marbles and the frieze of the Parthenon were all burnt into lime, and that the granite Egyptian statues were hewn and squared into building-stones, and that the mummies had all turned to dust two thousand years ago; and, in fine, that all the material relics of so many successive ages had disappeared with the generations that produced them.'

NATHANIEL HAWTHORNE, American novelist,
*English Notebooks*, 1854

## Covent Garden

'Covent-garden market, and the avenues leading to it, are thronged with carts of all sorts, sizes, and descriptions, from the heavy lumbering wagon, with its four stout horses, to the jingling costermonger's cart, with its consumptive donkey. The pavement is already strewed with decayed cabbage-leaves, broken hay-bands, and all the indescribable litter of a vegetable market; men are shouting, carts backing, horses neighing, boys fighting, basket-women talking, piemen expatiating on the excellence of their pastry, and donkeys braying.'

CHARLES DICKENS, novelist, *Sketches by Boz*, 1836

## The Strand

'In one single street, named the Strand, leading to St Paul's, there are fifty-two goldsmith's shops, so rich and full of silver vessels, great and small, that in all the shops in Milan, Rome, Venice, and Florence put together, I do not think there would be found so many of the magnificence that are to be seen in London.'

ANDREAS TREVISAN, Venetian diplomat, 1498

'Full of pits and sloughs, very perilous … very noyous and foul, and in many places thereof very jeopardous to all people passing and repassing, as well on horseback as on foot.'

Description of the Strand in the Rolls of Parliament, 1540s

## Kensington Gardens

'In this lone, open glade I lie,
Screen'd by deep boughs on either hand;
And at its end, to stay the eye,
Those black-crown'd, red-boled pine-trees stand!
Birds here make song, each bird has his,
Across the girdling city's hum.
How green under the boughs it is!
How thick the tremulous sheep-cries come! …

'Calm soul of all things! make it mine
To feel, amid the city's jar,
That there abides a peace of thine,
Man did not make, and cannot mar.'

MATTHEW ARNOLD, poet, 'Lines Written in
Kensington Gardens', 1852

## Trafalgar Square

'Now stiff on a pillar with a phallic air Nelson stylites in Trafalgar Square reminds the British what once they were.'

LAWRENCE DURRELL, novelist and poet, 1912–1990

'We lived near enough to London for visits as a treat. The drive up was on single-carriageway A roads, parking was no problem, and you were allowed to feed the pigeons in Trafalgar Square.'

NEVILLE MERRITT, contributor to the 'Today Generation' feature on London in the early 1960s, *Today*, BBC Radio 4, 2007

'Queen Elizabeth is a man! Prince Charles is a faggot! Winston Churchill was full of shit! Shakespeare's French!'

DAVID KESSLER trying to get arrested in Trafalgar Square, *An American Werewolf in London*, 1981

'Pigeons in Trafalgar Square are part of the London scene enjoyed by citizens and visitors alike. The Square's feral pigeons are sociable and intelligent creatures.'

TONY BANKS, politician and animal rights campaigner, 1943–2006

'The Nelson monument, with Lord Nelson, in a cocked hat, on its top, is very grand in its effect. All about the square there were sundry loungers, people looking at the bas-reliefs on Nelson's Column, children paddling in the reservoirs of the fountains; and, it being a sunny day, it was a cheerful and lightsome, as well as an impressive scene.'

NATHANIEL HAWTHORNE, American novelist,
*English Notebooks*, 1854

'We hear so much about the pigeons here. They are so friendly. Why do you want to get rid of them? We've heard of the British bulldog spirit but you should have pigeon spirit as well.'

American tourist, on the pigeon-feeding ban in
Trafalgar Square, BBC News, 2002

## Soho and the West End

'Oxford Street, stony-hearted stepmother, thou that listenest to the sighs of orphans and drinkest the tears of children.'

THOMAS DE QUINCEY, writer, *Confessions of an English Opium Eater*, 1822

'They emerged out of a narrow street and saw the early sunlight filling Leicester Square. It will never be known, I suppose, why this square itself should look so alien and in some ways so continental. It will never be known whether it was the foreign look that attracted the foreigners or the foreigners who gave it the foreign look.'

C K CHESTERTON, writer, *The Man Who Was Thursday*, 1908

'The lights down in hell will look just like that.'

GEORGE ORWELL, writer, describing Piccadilly Circus, *Keep the Aspidistra Flying*, 1936

'Complete separation between the streets and squares occupied by the nobility and gentry, and the meaner houses occupied by mechanics and the trading parts of the community.'

JOHN NASH, architect, on the advantages of the proposed Regent Street development, 1811

'Untidy, full of Greeks, Ishmaelites, cats, Italians, tomatoes, restaurants, organs, coloured stuffs, queer names …'

JOHN GALSWORTHY, novelist, describing Soho, *The Forsyte Saga: In Chancery*, 1920

## Buckingham Palace

'Buckingham Palace – a long building, in the Italian style, but of no impressiveness, and which one soon wearies of looking at.'

NATHANIEL HAWTHORNE, American novelist, *English Notebooks*, 1854

## Westminster Abbey

'That temple of silence and reconciliation where the enmities of twenty generations lie buried.'

THOMAS BABINGTON MACAULAY, politician and historian, 1843

'Stone seems, by winning labour of the chisel, to have been robbed of its density, suspended aloft, as if by magic.'

WASHINGTON IRVING, American writer, 1820s

## Westminster Bridge

'Earth has not anything to show more fair;
Dull would he be of soul who could pass by
A sight so touching in its majesty.
This city now doth like a garment wear
The beauty of the morning: silent, bare,
Ships, towers, domes, theatres, and temples lie
Open unto the fields, and to the sky –
All bright and glittering in the smokeless air.
Never did sun more beautifully steep
In his first splendour valley, rock, or hill;
Ne'er saw I, never felt, a calm so deep!
The river glideth at his own sweet will:
Dear God! the very houses seem asleep;
And all that mighty heart is lying still!'

WILLIAM WORDSWORTH, poet, 'Upon Westminster Bridge', 1802

# London
# People

LONDON IS A historic city of streets and buildings, but without the people who have inhabited it over the centuries there would be no streets, no buildings and no life. For all that the monuments of the great metropolis may impress commentators, it is often the citizens who leave the longest lasting impression.

'London landladies are Britannias armed with helmet, shield, trident, and have faces with the word "No" stamped like a coat of arms on them.'

V S PRITCHETT, writer, 1900–1997

'I stopped at a tavern in the Strand, the waiter of which observed to me, "They say Sebastopol is taken, sir!" It was only such an interesting event that could have induced an English waiter to make a remark to a stranger, not called for in the way of business.'

NATHANIEL HAWTHORNE, American novelist,
*English Notebooks*, 1854

'But now behold,
In the quick forge and working-house of thought,
How London doth pour out her citizens.
The mayor and all his brethren in best sort,
Like to the senators of the antique Rome,
With the plebeians swarming at their heels.'

WILLIAM SHAKESPEARE, playwright, *Henry V*, 1599

'A man in court dress cannot walk the streets of London without being pelted with mud by the mob … the Londoners hoot the king and the royal family when they appear in public.'

GIACOMO CASANOVA, Italian adventurer, remembering London in the 1760s, *Memoirs: Volume 22: To London*, 1725–1798

'War or anything that seems likely to lead to war is always popular with the London mob.'

HERBERT ASQUITH, Prime Minister, 1914

'The appearance of the people in the streets of London is one of the first things that attract the notice of strangers. The native inhabitants ... are somewhat under middle size, but their limbs and features are generally well formed. They are of spare habit, but rather muscular; they are characterised by firmness of carriage, and an erect, independent air; they move with a measured step, and generally at a very brisk pace. The features are generally very strong marked, and pointed; the eye in particular presents an openness and fullness that is remarkable. The tout-ensemble of the countenance bears an air of keenness, animation and intelligence, that distinguish the Londoner from his country neighbour.'

JOHN HOGG, naturalist, 1837

'All in tumult and hurry; one would imagine that they were impelled by some disorder of the brain, that will not suffer them to be at rest ... How can I help supposing they are actually possessed by a spirit, more absurd and pernicious than anything we meet within the bounds of Bedlam?'

TOBIAS SMOLLETT, novelist, description of Londoners from *The Expedition of Humphry Clinker*, 1771

'You will recognise, my boy, the first sign of age: it is when you go out into the streets of London and realise for the first time how young the policemen look.'

SEYMOUR HICKS, actor, 1871–1949

'It is strange to see how many people are aiming at the small change in your pocket. In every square a beggar-woman meets you, and turns back to follow your steps with her miserable murmur. At the street-crossings there are old men or little girls with their brooms; urchins propose to brush your boots; and if you get into a cab, a man runs to open the door for you, and touches his hat for a fee, as he closes it again.'

NATHANIEL HAWTHORNE, American novelist,
*English Notebooks*, 1853

'And outside the Abbey, hawkers innumerable selling penny-mementoes of "the late Irving" – driving their own humbler trade over the tomb. And, as I jumped into a hansom, "Don't forget the linkman today, sir. He's been *very* attentive." Funerals ought not to be held in so commercial a place as London.'

MAX BEERBOHM, writer and artist, attending Sir Henry Irving's
funeral at Westminster Abbey, 1905

'I wander through each chartered street,
Near where the chartered Thames docs flow,
And mark in every face I meet,
Marks of weakness, marks of woe.
In every cry of every man,
In every infant's cry of fear,
In every voice, in every ban,
The mind-forged manacles I hear:
How the chimney-sweeper's cry
Every blackening church appals,
And the hapless soldier's sigh
Runs in blood down palace-walls.
But most, through midnight streets I hear
How the youthful harlot's curse
Blasts the new-born infant's tear,
And blights with plagues the marriage-hearse.'

WILLIAM BLAKE, poet, 'London', 1792

'The [Londoners'] attitude to foreigners is like the attitude
to dogs: dogs are neither human nor British, but so long
as you keep them under control, give them their exercise,
feed them, pat them, you will find their wild emotions are
amusing, and their characters interesting.'

V S PRITCHETT, author, 1900–1997

'There are certain descriptions of people who, oddly enough, appear to appertain exclusively to the metropolis. You meet them, every day, in the streets of London, but no one ever encounters them elsewhere; they seem indigenous to the soil, and to belong as exclusively to London as its own smoke, or the dingy bricks and mortar. We could illustrate the remark by a variety of examples, but, in our present sketch, we will only advert to one class as a specimen – that class which is so aptly and expressively designated as "shabby-genteel".'

CHARLES DICKENS, novelist, *Sketches by Boz*, 1836

'The final sideshow, when one has done the superb museums and art galleries, the cathedrals and churches, the libraries and monuments, the Zoo, Hampstead Heath on Bank Holiday, the Cup Final, is the population of eccentrics … Our public eccentrics are not exhibitionists, they are not trying to draw a crowd – as happened often in Paris. They are doing the very opposite: they are – and we understand this – withdrawn deeply into private life.'

V S PRITCHETT, author, *London Perceived*, 1962

'I suppose the world has heard of the famous Solomon Eagle, an enthusiast. He, though not infected at all but in his head, went about denouncing of judgment upon the city in a frightful manner, sometimes quite naked, and with a pan of burning charcoal on his head.'

DANIEL DEFOE, novelist, *A Journal of the Plague Year*, 1722

'I used to pass a dwarf, dressed in old clothes and with wizened features, who in a hoarse voice would direct the traffic at the crossroads of Theobald's Road and Grays Inn Road; he was there every day and then suddenly, in the summer of 1978, he was gone.'

PETER ACKROYD, novelist and historian,
*London: The Biography*, 2000

'I think London's sexy because it's so full of eccentrics.'

RACHEL WEISZ, actor, b. 1970

'Don't talk to me about London. Plenty people there have heart like stone. Any complaint – the answer is "prove it".'

JEAN RHYS, novelist, *Let Them Call It Jazz*, 1968

'If it were not for the human life and bustle of London, it would be a very stupid place, with a heavy and dreary monotony of unpicturesque streets.'

NATHANIEL HAWTHORNE, American novelist,
*English Notebooks*, 1853

'I love dis great polluted place
Where pop stars come to live their dreams
Here ravers come for drum and bass
And politicians plan their schemes,
The music of the world is here
Dis city can play any song
They came to here from everywhere
Tis they that made dis city strong.'

BENJAMIN ZEPHANIAH, poet, 'The London Breed', 1998

# London
# Power

SINCE ITS EARLIEST days, London has been the most powerful city in the kingdom. As well as being the cultural and trading capital of the nation, it is also the seat of our Parliament – and the doings of MPs and ministers of the crown have long been a subject of fascination for many Londoners.

'The city is delightful indeed, when it has a good governor.'

WILLIAM FITZSTEPHEN, monk, 1180

'It is the folly of too many to mistake the echo of a London coffee-house for the voice of the kingdom.'

JONATHAN SWIFT, Irish writer, 1667–1745

'The members of the English Parliament are fond of comparing themselves to the old Romans ... There is in London a senate, some of the members whereof are accused (doubtless very unjustly) of selling their voices on certain occasions, as was done in Rome; this is the only resemblance.'

VOLTAIRE, French writer and philosopher, *Letters on England*, 1733

'The British Parliament – the perfection of a stupendous institution, I know, and the admiration of all surrounding nations and succeeding ages, I do not doubt, but perhaps a little the better now and then for being pricked up to its work.'

CHARLES DICKENS, novelist, *The Uncommercial Traveller*, 1869

'I never saw so many shocking bad hats in my life.'

THE DUKE OF WELLINGTON, on seeing the first Reformed Parliament, 1832

'London is extremely improved ... Now for the first time, it has the air of a seat of Government, and not of an immeasurable metropolis of "shopkeepers" to use Napoleon's expression.'

PRINCE PÜCKLER-MUSKAU, German nobleman, 1826

'That splendid theatre of pitiful passion.'

SIR ROBERT WALPOLE, politician, describing the House of Commons, 1767

'The body of the House and the side galleries are full of Members; some, with their legs on the back of the opposite seat; some, with theirs stretched out to their utmost length on the floor; some going out, others coming in; all talking, laughing, lounging, coughing, oh-ing, questioning, or groaning; presenting a conglomeration of noise and confusion, to be met with in no other place in existence, not even excepting Smithfield on a market-day, or a cock-pit in its glory.'

CHARLES DICKENS, novelist, visits the House of Commons,
*Sketches by Boz*, 1836

'All reputations are made swiftly on the banks of the Thames and as quickly lost.'

FRANÇOIS-RENÉ, vicomte de Chateaubriand,
French writer and diplomat, 1850

'I've been doing nineteen hours a day on London, nothing else, I mean this has been my whole life, and writing has been put on one side, and if I'm privileged enough to be the Mayor of this city, then I will not write again.'

JEFFREY ARCHER, writer and politician,
when running for Mayor of London, 1999

'I think … that it is the best club in London.'

> CHARLES DICKENS, novelist, on the
> House of Commons, *Our Mutual Friend*, 1865

'I want to be Prime Minister, but I will stand for Mayor of London first.'

> MOHAMED AL-FAYED, businessman and
> former owner of Harrods, b. 1933

'London … has resisted absolutism and maintained the rights of the citizens within the state … It has never been of greater importance than now that these ideals should continue to exist, in one country at least, in Europe.'

> STEEN EILER RASMUSSEN, writer and architect, 1937

'The problem is that many MPs never see the London that exists beyond the wine bars and brothels of Westminster.'

> KEN LIVINGSTONE, politician, b. 1945

# London
# Pleasure

FROM SIMPLE STREET entertainers to great theatres, from the casinos to the brothels, London has always been a city of innumerable diversions, and its citizens are often remarked upon for their enthusiastic, if not to say maniacal, pursuit of pleasure. London serves to satisfy even the lustiest appetite, whether Londoners are hungering for entertainment, sex or the joys of life itself.

'Tumblers, hand-organists, puppet-showmen, bagpipers, and all such vagrant mirth-makers, are very numerous in the streets of London.'

NATHANIEL HAWTHORNE, American novelist,
*English Notebooks*, 1854

'It is impossible to overestimate the thirst for spectacle among Londoners through many centuries.'

PETER ACKROYD, novelist and historian,
*London: The Biography*, 2000

'The pleasures of a town life, the daily round from the tavern to the play, from the play to the coffee-house, from the coffee-house to the _____, are within the reach of every man who is, regardless of his health, his money, and his company.'

EDWARD GIBBON, historian, 1796

'The most striking thing to a foreigner in English theatres is the unheard-of coarseness and brutality of the audiences.'

PRINCE PÜCKLER-MUSKAU, German nobleman, 1827

'The English plays are like their English puddings: nobody has any taste for them but themselves.'

VOLTAIRE, French writer and philosopher, 1694–1778

'Go on writing plays, my boy. One of these days one of these London producers will go into his office and say to his secretary, "Is there a play from Shaw this morning?" and when she says, "No," he will say, "Well, then we'll have to start on the rubbish." And that's your chance, my boy.'

GEORGE BERNARD SHAW, Irish playwright
and essayist, 1856–1950

'People are there forbidden to work or take any recreation on that day [Sunday], in which the severity is twice as great as that of the Romish Church. No operas, plays, or concerts are allowed in London on Sundays, and even cards are so expressly forbidden that none but persons of quality, and those we call the genteel, play on that day; the rest of the nation go either to church, to the tavern, or to see their mistresses.'

VOLTAIRE, French philosopher, *Letters on England*, 1734

'It was the dead hour of Sunday morning, midway in service-time, and long before the opening of public-houses. In the neighbourhood of those places of refreshment were occasionally found small groups of men and boys, standing with their hands in their pockets, dispirited, seldom caring even to smoke; they kicked their heels against the kerbstone and sighed for one o'clock.'

GEORGE GISSING, novelist, *The Nether World*, 1889

'Forasmuch as there is great noise in the city caused by hustling over large balls, from which many evils may arise, which God forbid, we command and forbid on behalf of the King, on pain of imprisonment, such game to be used in the city in future.'

Proclamation of EDWARD II banning football from the streets of London, 1314

'One class of men in London appear to have no enjoyment beyond leaning against posts. We never saw a regular bricklayer's labourer take any other recreation, fighting excepted.'

CHARLES DICKENS, novelist, *Sketches by Boz*, 1836

'The pub that I use most often, the Queensbury in north London, is absolutely thriving. It's near home and near the train station, it has a nice garden and it does nice food, but above that, the significance for me is that it used to be the offices of the Brent Conservative Club. Each drink I consume in there is viewed as a triumph over vanquished opponents.'

KEN LIVINGSTONE, politician, *The Guardian*, 2011

'Once I went into a "casino". The music was blaring, people were dancing, a huge crowd was milling round. The place was magnificently decorated. But gloom never forsakes the English even in the midst of gaiety; even when they dance they look serious, not to say sullen, making hardly any steps and then only as if in execution of some duty.'

FYODOR DOSTOEVSKY, Russian novelist, *Winter Notes on Summer Impressions*, 1863

'A broken heart is a very pleasant complaint for a man in London if he has a comfortable income.'

GEORGE BERNARD SHAW, Irish playwright, *Man and Superman*, 1903

'Londoners are characteristically lenient in matters of sexual impropriety. How can they be otherwise in a city where every form of vice and extravagance is continually available?'

PETER ACKROYD, novelist and historian,
*London: The Biography*, 2000

'London, what are thy suburbs but licensed stews? Can it be so many brothel-houses of salary sensuality and six-penny whoredom (the next door to the magistrates) should be set up and maintained, if bribes did not bestir them? I accuse none, but certainly justice somewhere is corrupted.

'Whole hospitals of ten-times-a-day dishonested strumpets have we cloistered together. Night and day the entrance unto them is as free as to a tavern. Not one of them hath but a hundred retainers. Prentices and poor servants they encourage to rob their masters. Gentleman's purses and pockets the will dive into and pick, even while they are dallying with them.'

THOMAS NASHE, poet and author, 1594

'As a heap of rubbish will ferment, so surely will a number of unvirtuous women.'

WILLIAM ACTON, doctor and author, *Prostitution*, 1857

'There are no women in the world so beautiful as the English.'

FYODOR DOSTOEVSKY, Russian novelist,
*Winter Notes on Summer Impressions*, 1863

'Last night … I met a monstrous big whore in the Strand, whom I had a great curiosity to lubricate.'

JAMES BOSWELL, writer and frequenter of prostitutes, 1762

# London Society

BEFORE THE TWENTIETH century, the high life of the aristocracy defined the image of London among those who mattered – that is to say, the aristocracy themselves. The social round of court and the season may have been glittering social occasions to cherish for most who attended, but even at the time there were those who would have preferred to spend their time in other ways.

'The man who can dominate a London dinner table can dominate the world.'

OSCAR WILDE, Irish writer and poet,
*A Woman of No Importance*, 1893

'I do not think there is anything deserving the name of society to be found out of London.'

WILLIAM HAZLITT, writer, 1778–1830

'Last night, party at Lansdowne House. Tonight, party at Lady Charlotte Greville's – deplorable waste of time, and something of temper. Nothing imparted – nothing acquired – talking without ideas – if any thing like thought in my mind, it was not on the subjects on which we were gabbling. Heigho! and in this way half London pass what is called life.'

LORD BYRON, poet, 1788–1824

'I became the toast of London. A lot of people I met came from these really decadent families where the married men were gay and no one thought anything about it.'

ROBERT MAPPLETHORPE, American photographer, 1946–1989

'A man may learn from his Bible to be a more thorough gentleman than if he had been brought up in all the drawing rooms in London.'

CHARLES KINGSLEY, novelist and clergyman, 1819–1875

'Who's your fat friend?'

BEAU BRUMMELL, dandy, referring to the Prince of Wales, later George IV, from *Life of George Brummell* by Captain William Jesse, 1844

'The day was thus distributed in London: at six o'clock in the morning, one hastened to a party of pleasure, consisting of a breakfast in the country; one returned to London; one changed one's dress to walk in Bond Street or Hyde Park; one dressed again to dine at half-past seven; one dressed again for the opera; at midnight, one dressed once more for an evening party or rout. What a life of enchantment! I should a hundred times have preferred the galleys.'

FRANÇOIS-RENÉ, vicomte de Chateaubriand,
French writer and diplomat, 1850

'I wish I could know exactly what the English style good conversation. Probably it is something like plum-pudding – as heavy, but seldom so rich.'

NATHANIEL HAWTHORNE, American novelist,
*English Notebooks*, 1854

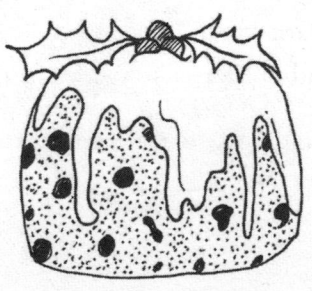

'The hierarchy of class in London was rigid. It was like a religion. It still is to a certain extent.'

SIR BEN KINGSLEY, actor, b. 1943

'Can't make out how you stand London Society. The thing has gone to the dogs, a lot of damned nobodies talking about nothing.'

LORD CAVERSHAM in *An Ideal Husband* by Oscar Wilde, 1895

'I love London society! I think it has immensely improved. It is entirely composed now of beautiful idiots and brilliant lunatics. Just what Society should be.'

MABEL CHILTERN in *An Ideal Husband* by Oscar Wilde, 1895

'In Paris, you learn wit; in London, you learn to crush your social rivals; and in Florence, you learn poise.'

VIRGIL THOMSON, American composer, 1896–1989

'If you lived in London, where the whole system is one of false good-fellowship, and you may know a man for twenty years without finding out that he hates you like poison, you would soon have your eyes opened. There we do unkind things in a kind way: we say bitter things in a sweet voice: we always give our friends chloroform when we tear them to pieces.'

GEORGE BERNARD SHAW, Irish playwright,
*You Never Can Tell*, 1897

# London
# Poverty

DESPITE THE BEST efforts of London's 'better' classes to ignore and criminalise the lesser citizens over many centuries, the London poor have long been emblematic of the city. The raucous vitality of the rookeries, the hard-working stoicism of the labouring classes and the famous community spirit of the East End are as significant in defining London as any great cathedral or palace.

'There are such great multitudes of people brought to inhabit in small rooms, whereof a great part are seen very poor, yea, such as must live by begging, or by worse means, and they heaped up together, and in a sort smothered with many families of children and servants in one house or small tenement.'

Proclamation of ELIZABETH I, 1580

'One might mark the years and epochs by the successive kinds of exiles that walk London streets and, in grim silent manner, demand pity from us and reflections from us.'

THOMAS CARLYLE, historian, 1795–1881

'In London the masses can be seen on a scale and in conditions not to be seen anywhere else in the world.'

FYODOR DOSTOEVSKY, Russian novelist,
*Winter Notes on Summer Impressions*, 1863

'The London poor: least original and least articulate beings within the confines of civilisation.'

GEORGE GISSING, novelist, *The Nether World*, 1889

'Of that period [the mid-nineteenth century] it is to be said that there is none in the history of London in which less regard was shown for the conditions of the great mass of the inhabitants of the metropolis.'

HENRY JEPHSON, historian,
*The Sanitary Evolution of London*, 1907

'I have seen the Polynesian savage in his primitive condition, before the missionary or blackbirder or the beachcomber got at him. With all his savagery he was not half so savage, so unclean, so irreclaimable, as the tenant of a tenement in an East London slum.'

THOMAS HUXLEY, biologist, 1825–1895

'The East End is a vast city, as famous in its way as any the hand of man has made. But who knows the East End? It is down through Cornhill and out beyond Leadenhall Street and Aldgate Pump, one will say: a shocking place, where he once went with a curate; an evil plexus of slums that hide human creeping things; where filthy men and women live on penn'orths of gin, whence collars and clean shirts are decencies unknown, where every citizen wears a black eye, and none ever combs his hair. The East End is a place, says another, which is given over to the Unemployed. And the Unemployed is a race whose token is a clay pipe, and whose enemy is soap.'

ARTHUR MORRISON, novelist, *Tales of Mean Streets*, 1894

'About the London shop girls of the meaner sort no derogatory remarks can be too strong, just as no commendation can be too high of the courtesy, honest, and good nature of the girls who wait on you in the shops on Oxford and Bond Streets.

'This court-born, alley-nursed, street-bred girl is everywhere. Sometimes she is sober, oftener she is not. She sells you flowers and fruit on every corner, serves in bars and cheap eating-houses. We have nothing at all at home to correspond to her ... She wears flowers and paste jewels, but she seldom bathes, never has enough hairpins, and considers toothbrushes necessary only for members of the royal family.'

WILLA CATHER, novelist, *Willa Cather in Europe*, 1902

'The aged, the orphan, the halt, the blind of London would fill an ordinary city.'

BLANCHARD JERROLD, writer, *London: A Pilgrimage*, 1872

# London's River

FROM THE CITY'S beginning through to our own century, the Thames has been central to London life – at times to an extent that is now difficult to imagine. Main port of the nation, main highway and main sewer of the city: the capital's river was all these things, as these quotes remind us.

'Above all ryvers thy Ryver hath renowne,
Whose beryall stremys, plesaunt and preclare,
Under lusty wallys renneth down,
Where many a swanne doth swymme with wyngis fare;
Where many a barge doth saile, and row with are,
Where many a ship doth rest with toppe-royall.
O! Towne of townes, patrone and not-compare:
London, thou art the floure of Cities all.'

WILLIAM DUNBAR, poet, 'To the City of London', *c*. 1500

'The Thames is not so wide and majestic as I had imagined – nothing like the Mersey, for example. As a picturesque object, however, flowing through the midst of a city, it would lose by any increase of width.'

NATHANIEL HAWTHORNE, American novelist,
*English Notebooks*, 1853

'Even though I knew the Thames is a small river compared with the great ones of the world, I would patriotically make it wider and wider in my mind.'

V S PRITCHETT, author, *A Cab at the Door*, 1968

'Thames, the most loved of all Ocean's sons,
By his old sire, to his embraces runs,
Hasting to pay his tribute to the Sea,
Like mortal life to meet eternity.'

JOHN DENHAM, poet, 'Cooper's Hill', 1642

'A Stygian pool reeking with ineffable and unbearable horror.'

BENJAMIN DISRAELI, Prime Minister, 1858

'Sweet Thames, run softly, till I end my song.'

EDMUND SPENSER, poet, 'Prothalamion', 1596

'The river had an awful look, the buildings on the banks were muffled in black shrouds, and the reflected lights seemed to originate deep in the water, as if the spectres of suicides were holding them to show where they went down. The wild moon and clouds were as restless as an evil conscience in a tumbled bed, and the very shadow of the immensity of London seemed to lie oppressively upon the river.'

CHARLES DICKENS, novelist, *The Uncommercial Traveller*, 1869

'We got on board one of these [pleasure steamers], not very well knowing, nor much caring, whither it might take us, and steamed down the river, which is bordered with the shabbiest, blackest, ugliest, meanest buildings: it is the back side of the town; and, in truth, the muddy tide of the Thames deserves to see no better.'

NATHANIEL HAWTHORNE, American novelist,
*English Notebooks*, 1853

'But thank God! The Thames is between me and the Duchess of Queensbury.'

HORACE WALPOLE, writer, 1747

'In June 1858 ... an exceptionally hot summer and unusually low rainfall combined to produce what all London knew as "The Great Stink". Parliament was in a good position to appreciate the nuisance, for the windows had to be draped with curtains soaked in chloride of lime so that members could breathe. To cross Westminster Bridge, it was necessary to hold a handkerchief firmly over one's nose and mouth and those who travelled on the river steamers suffered greatly when the paddles churned the water into stinking eddies.'

R J MITCHELL and M D R LEYS, authors,
*A History of London Life*, 1958

'If Mr Gladstone fell into the Thames, that would be a misfortune. If someone were to pull him out, that would be a calamity.'

BENJAMIN DISRAELI, novelist and Prime Minister,
explaining the difference between a misfortune
and a calamity, 1804–1881

'The docks are impossible to describe. They are unbelievable! Tyre and Carthage all rolled into one!'

PAUL VERLAINE, French poet, 1872

'The muddy tide of the Thames, reflecting nothing, and hiding a million unclean secrets within its breast – a sort of guilty conscience as it were, unwholesome with the rivulets of sin that constantly flow into it.'

NATHANIEL HAWTHORNE, American novelist,
*Our Old Home*, 1863

'The river divides London not just physically but socially: north of the river is the posh side, the south very definitely isn't. I know this because I come from the south.'

SIR MICHAEL CAINE, actor,
*What's It All About?*, 1992

'The yellow leaves begin to fade
And flutter from the Temple elms,
And at my feet the pale green Thames
Lies like a rod of rippled jade.'

Oscar Wilde, poet, 'Symphony in Yellow', 1889

'He walked on the Embankment once under a dark red sunset. The red river reflected the red sky, and they both reflected his anger. The sky, indeed, was so swarthy, and the light on the river so lurid, that the water almost seemed of fiercer flame than the sunset it mirrored. It looked like a stream of literal fire winding under the vast caverns of the subterranean country.'

G K CHESTERTON, writer, *The Man Who Was Thursday*, 1908

'The Mississippi is muddy water, but the Thames is liquid history.'

JOHN BURNS, politician, defending the Thames from a negative comparison with the Mississippi, 1929

# London
# Life

LIVING IN LONDON is about the experience of being there, feeling oneself surrounded by the great city, and becoming part of the unceasing flow of life that sustains it. For many, this has led to a feeling of a transcendent sense of belonging – while others find only irritation and despair.

Yet that is the true heart of London: its diversity, its polar opposites nestling side by side, its thrusting, sink-or-swim opportunity-grabbing attitude that determinedly makes its mark on its residents, and leaves them forever changed. London is an expensive, complex place, but it is also rich in all the experiences it has to offer.

'London doesn't love the latent or the lurking, has neither time, nor taste, nor sense for anything less discernible than the red flag in front of the steam-roller. It wants cash over the counter and letters ten feet high.'

HENRY JAMES, American novelist, 1843–1916

'You are now
In London, that great sea, whose ebb and flow
At once is deaf and loud, and on the shore
Vomits its wrecks, and still howls on for more.
Yet in its depth what treasures!'

PERCY BYSSHE SHELLEY, poet, 'Letter to Maria Gisborne', 1820

'Why Sir, you find no man, at all intellectual, who is willing to leave London. No, Sir, when a man is tired of London, he is tired of life; for there is in London all that life can afford.'

SAMUEL JOHNSON, writer and polymath,
in Boswell's *Life of Johnson*, 1791

'The truth is that in London it is always a sickly season. Nobody is healthy in London, nobody can be.'

JANE AUSTEN, novelist, *Emma*, 1815

'Here, Wisdom calls: "Seek Virtue first, be bold!
As Gold is to Silver, Virtue is to Gold."
There, London's voice: "Get Money, Money Still!
And let Virtue follow, if she will."'

ALEXANDER POPE, poet, 'Imitations of Horace', 1738

'London is a modern Babylon.'

BENJAMIN DISRAELI, politician and novelist, *Tancred*, 1847

'Crowds without company, dissipation without pleasure.'

EDWARD GIBBON, historian, 1737–1794

'London is a small place, and it is very incestuous. People know where you live. Everybody is sort of on top of each other.'

JEANETTE WINTERSON, novelist, b. 1959

'I do notice that when I've been away and I come back to London. People look at you. People are ready to pick arguments.'

COLIN FIRTH, actor, b. 1960

'I have passed all my days in London, until I have formed as many and intense local attachments, as any of your mountaineers can have done with dead nature. The Lighted shops of the Strand and Fleet Street, the innumerable trades, tradesmen and customers, coaches, wagons, playhouses, all the bustle and wickedness round about Covent Garden, the very women of the Town, the watchmen, drunken scenes, rattles – life awake, if you awake, at all hours of the night, the impossibility of being dull in Fleet Street, the crowds, the very dirt and mud, the Sun shining upon houses and pavements, the print shops, the old book stalls, parsons cheap'ning books, coffee houses, steams of soup from kitchens, the pantomimes, London itself a pantomime and a masquerade – all these things work themselves into my mind and feed me without a power of satiating me. The wonder of these sights impels me into nightwalks, and I often shed tears in the motley Strand from fullness of joy at so much Life.'

CHARLES LAMB, writer, 1801

'Nothing is certain in London but expense.'

WILLIAM SHENSTONE, poet, 1714–1763

'As to London, we must console ourselves with the thought that if life outside is less poetic than it was in the days of old, inwardly its poetry is much deeper.'

GOLDWIN SMITH, historian, 1823–1910

'The pleasure of my life as an office boy lay in being one of the London crowd.'

V S PRITCHETT, author, *A Cab at the Door,* 1968

'By seeing London, I have seen as much of life as the world can show.'

SAMUEL JOHNSON, writer and polymath, in Boswell's
*Life of Johnson,* 1791

'There was a size, a richness, about London. You could find anything or anybody you wanted in it, and you could also hide in it.'

J B PRIESTLEY, novelist and playwright, *Angel Pavement,* 1930

'The noise, the crowd, the glare of the shops and signs agreeably confused me.'

JAMES BOSWELL, diarist, *London Journal*, 1762–1763

'It is true, too, that you can only be happy in London if you begin to consider yourself a Londoner. It is the secret of successful assimilation.'

PETER ACKROYD, novelist and historian,
*London: The Biography*, 2000

'It never misses, it never can miss anyone. It loves nobody, it needs nobody; it tolerates all the types of mankind.'

FORD MADOX FORD, novelist, *The Soul of London*, 1905

'London is a splendid place to live in for those who can get out of it.'

GEORGE JOHN GORDON BRUCE, 7th Lord Balfour of Burleigh,
*The Observer*, 1944

'The only inconveniences of London are, the immoderate drinking of foolish persons, and the frequent fires.'

WILLIAM FITZSTEPHEN, monk, *c.* 1180

# London
# Food & Drink

HISTORICALLY, LONDON HAS never been seen as a centre of culinary excellence – yet the appetite and gusto of its inhabitants have never been in doubt. The peculiar singularities of London's hospitality industry, meanwhile, have been the cause of frequent amusement, and occasional horror, over the centuries.

'Would I were in an alehouse in London. I would give all my fame for a pot of ale, and safety.'

WILLIAM SHAKESPEARE,
playwright, *Henry V*, 1599

'The English probably eat with more simple enjoyment than any other people; not ravenously, as we often do, and not exquisitely and artificially, like the French, but deliberately and vigorously, and with due absorption in the business, so that nothing good is lost upon them.'

NATHANIEL HAWTHORNE, American novelist,
*English Notebooks*, 1854

'Whenever I go to bars in London, people send me over Cosmopolitans. It's a very sweet gesture, but I don't like them, so they just sit there.'

KIM CATTRALL, actor and *Sex and the City* star, b. 1956

'In London there are a great number of coffee-houses, most of which, to tell the truth, are not over clean or well furnished, owing to the quantity of people who resort to these places and because of the smoke, which would quickly destroy good furniture.

'Englishmen are great drinkers. In these coffee-houses you can partake of chocolate, tea, or coffee, and of all sorts of liquors, served hot; also in many places you can have wine, punch, or ale …

'What attracts enormously in these coffee-houses are the gazettes and other public papers. All Englishmen are great newsmongers. Workmen habitually begin the day by going to coffee-rooms in order to read the latest news. I have often seen shoeblacks and other persons of that class club together to purchase a farthing paper … Some coffee-houses are a resort for learned scholars and for wits; others are the resort of dandies or of politicians, or again of professional newsmongers.'

CÉSAR DE SAUSSURE, Swiss traveller, 1727

'I was seeing arrive the day when London restaurants, whose badness is literally fabulous, would become impossible, and the feeding question a problem so grave as to drive me from the land.'

HENRY JAMES, American novelist, in a letter to his father, 13 February 1877

'A new kind of drunkenness, unknown to our ancestors, is lately sprung up among us, and which, if not put a stop to, will infallibly destroy a great part of the inferior people. The drunkenness I here intend is … by this Poison called Gin … the principal sustenance (if it may be so called) of more than a hundred thousand People in this Metropolis.'

HENRY FIELDING, novelist and magistrate, *An Enquiry into the Causes of the Late Increase of Robbers*, 1751

'The gin-shops in and near Drury-Lane, Holborn, St Giles's, Covent-garden, and Clare-market, are the handsomest in London. There is more of filth and squalid misery near those great thorough-fares than in any part of this mighty city.'

CHARLES DICKENS, novelist, *Sketches by Boz*, 1836

'If I would drink water, I must quaff the mawkish contents of an open aqueduct, exposed to all manner of defilement, or swallow that which comes from the river Thames, impregnated with all the filth that is London and Westminster. Human excrement is the least offensive part of the concrete, which is comprised of all the drugs, minerals and poisons used in mechanics and manufactures, enriched with the putrefying carcasses of beasts and men, and mixed with the scouring of all the wash-tubs, kennels, and common sewers within the bills of mortality.

'This is the agreeable potation extolled by the Londoners as the finest water in the universe.'

TOBIAS SMOLLETT, novelist,
*The Expedition of Humphry Clinker*, 1771

'Foreigners remarked that the coffee-house was that which especially distinguished London from all other cities; that the coffee-house was the Londoner's home, and that those who wished to find a gentleman commonly asked, not whether he lived in Fleet Street or Chancery Lane, but whether he frequented the Grecian or the Rainbow.'

THOMAS BABINGTON MACAULAY,
writer and politician, 1800–1859

'A beefsteak-house is a most excellent place to dine at. You come in there to a warm, comfortable, large room, where a number of people are sitting at table. You take whatever place you find empty; call for what you like, which you get well and cleverly dressed. Nobody minds you, and you pay very reasonably. My dinner (beef, bread and beer and waiter) was only a shilling.'

JAMES BOSWELL, diarist, 1762

'The bread I eat in London is a deleterious paste, mixed up with chalk, alum, and bone-ashes, insipid to the taste, and destructive to the constitution. The good people are not ignorant of this adulteration; but they prefer it to wholesome bread, because it is whiter than the meal of corn. Thus they sacrifice their taste and their health, and the lives of their tender infants, to a most absurd gratification of a misjudging eye; and the miller or baker is obliged to poison them and their families, in order to live by his profession.'

TOBIAS SMOLLETT, novelist,
*The Expedition of Humphry Clinker*, 1771

'On Saturday nights half a million working men and women and their children spread like the ocean all over [London], clustering particularly in certain districts, and celebrate their sabbath all night long until five o'clock in the morning, in other words guzzle and drink like beasts to make up for the whole week …

   'Everyone is drunk, but drunk joylessly, gloomily and heavily, and everyone is somehow strangely silent. Only curses and bloody brawls occasionally break that suspicious and oppressively sad silence … Everyone is in a hurry to drink himself into insensibility … wives in no way lag behind their husbands and all get drunk together, while children crawl and run about among them.'

FYODOR DOSTOEVSKY, Russian novelist,
*Winter Notes on Summer Impressions*, 1863

'The English have been burning everything for so long, and no one paid attention to them. But now there are guys like Marco Pierre White, Jamie Oliver, and Gordon Ramsay. The London restaurant scene is as vibrant as anywhere in the world – London, Paris, New York.'

MARIO BATALI, American chef, b. 1960

# London Style

FROM THE 1960s onwards, London has been acknowledged as one of the world's fashion capitals. Yet in fact it was ever thus, and visitors to the city have been struck by the elegance and style of its citizens since as early as the twelfth century AD.

'The citizens of London are universally held up for admiration and renown for the elegance of their manners and dress, and the delights of their tables.'

WILLIAM FITZSTEPHEN, monk, *c.* 1180

'The women have much more liberty than perhaps in any other place; they also know full well how to make use of it, for they go out dressed in exceedingly fine clothes, and give all their attention to their ruffs and stuffs, to such a degree indeed that, as I am informed, many a one does not hesitate to wear velvet in the streets, which is common with them, whilst at home perhaps they have not a piece of dry bread.'

JACOB RATHGEB, German diplomat, 1592

'I must tell you that in England there is a kind of native complaint, which is called a "*cold*". That is why you hardly ever see people wearing summer clothes.'

LEOPOLD MOZART, composer, 1764

'In 1822, the duty of the man of fashion was, at the first glance, to present an unhappy and ailing figure; he was expected to have something neglected about his person: long nails; beard worn neither full nor shaved, but seeming to have sprouted at a given moment by surprise, through forgetfulness, amid the preoccupations of despair; a waving lock of hair; a profound, sublime wandering and fatal glance; lips contracted in scorn of the human race; a heart bored, Byronian, drowned in disgust at the mystery of existence.'

FRANÇOIS-RENÉ, vicomte de Chateaubriand,
French writer and diplomat, 1822

'Probably there are not more second-hand clothes sold in London than in Paris, and yet the mass of the London population have a second-hand look which is not to be detected on the mass of the Parisian population. I think this is mainly because a Parisian workman does not in the least trouble himself about what is worn by a Parisian idler, but dresses in the way of his own class, and for his own comfort. In London, on the contrary, the fashions descend; and you never fully know how inconvenient or ridiculous a fashion is, until you see it in its last descent.'

CHARLES DICKENS, novelist, *The Uncommercial Traveller*, 1869

'Gentlemen never wear brown in London.'

LORD CURZON, statesman, 1859–1925

'When I was a teenager in Iceland people would throw rocks and shout abuse at me because they thought I was weird. I never got that in London no matter what I wore.'

BJÖRK, musician, b. 1965

'What we do have in London is a fantastic pool of talent coming through the colleges. We are the fashion world's incubator.'

ALEXANDER MCQUEEN, fashion designer, 1969–2010

'In London, nobody comments on what you wear – they think that's not important to you or your state of well-being.'

STEVEN BERKOFF, actor, b. 1937

'The young Japanese, especially, love to wear the latest thing and when they come to London, they head for my shops as part of what they want to find in Britain.'

VIVIENNE WESTWOOD, fashion designer, b. 1941

'I was fourteen when I started modelling. At the end of that first day, my mum said, "If you want to do this, you're on your own because I'm not traipsing around London ever again like that. It's a nightmare."'

KATE MOSS, model, b. 1974

'I love London – it has so much energy.'

DONATELLA VERSACE, Italian fashion designer, b. 1955

'There are many LFW [London Fashion Week] designers producing eveningwear so covetable that you would consider selling an elderly relative … to own a piece.'

KELLY BOWERBANK, fashion editor, in *The Guardian*, 2010

'The reason I came to London was to buy a pair of Vivienne Westwood shoes.'

MEG MATHEWS, celebrity, in a radio interview, 2012

# London
# Celebrity

AS THE CULTURAL capital of the
United Kingdom, London has produced
more than its fair share of celebrities, as
well as constantly attracting famous and
glamorous visitors from around the world.
Here they share their insights with us.

'I love going into the centre of London because people don't give a monkey's about you or who you are. You can be in a restaurant and no one notices you, or if they do, they won't show it.'

TEDDY SHERINGHAM, footballer, b. 1966

'A lot of people basically are obsessed with the missus and I don't know really … she's just a bird from South London.'

PETE DOHERTY, musician, on Kate Moss, b. 1979

'I'm from New York so I feel very at home in London. It's like a metropolitan breeding ground for culture, art and diversity. I was very moved by how accepted I was there. There was definitely less need to wear my big sunglasses.'

SCARLETT JOHANSSON, American actor, b. 1984

'I think England has served me very well. I like living in London. I have absolutely no intentions of cutting those ties. There is absolutely no reason to do so. Certainly not so that I can have a swimming pool and a palm tree.'

COLIN FIRTH, actor, b. 1960

'I thought Cambridge was in London.'

JADE GOODY, reality TV star, 1981–2009

'I would rather start out somewhere small, like London or England.'

BRITNEY SPEARS, musician, b. 1981

'I go to London, my favourite city in the world, and I feel at home.'

BORIS BECKER, tennis legend, b. 1967

'I had to have some balls to be Irish Catholic in South London. Most of that time I spent fighting.'

PIERCE BROSNAN, actor, b. 1953

'When I was flying to Rome, we flew over London; I felt like bursting into tears. It's part of me, so I can't leave London behind for good.'

ROBERT PATTINSON, actor, b. 1986

'I'm incredibly boring; I had a very happy childhood. I never starved, nor did I have a silver spoon in my mouth. I'm one of those terribly middle-of-the-road, British middle class, South London gents.'

JUDE LAW, actor, b. 1972

'I was born in London, so going there is always a treat.'

SIR ROGER MOORE, actor, b. 1927

# London Compared

ALTHOUGH FOR MANY people London blots out all thoughts of other cities, some have thought to draw comparisons between our capital and those of other nations – usually not to London's credit.

'The shabbiness of our English capital, as compared with Paris, Bordeaux, Frankfurt, Milan, Geneva – almost any important town on the continent of Europe – I find very striking ... London is shabby in contrast with Edinburgh, with Aberdeen, with Exeter, with Liverpool, with a bright little town like Bury St Edmunds. London is shabby in contrast with New York, with Boston, with Philadelphia ... London is shabby by daylight, and shabbier by gaslight ... The mass of London people are shabby.'

CHARLES DICKENS, novelist, *The Uncommercial Traveller*, 1869

'The man who has stood on the Acropolis,
And looked down over Attica; or he
Who has sailed where picturesque Constantinople is,
Or seen Timbuctoo, or hath taken tea
In small-eyed China's crockery-ware metropolis,
Or sat amidst the bricks of Nineveh,
May not think much of London's first appearance –
But ask him what he thinks of it a year hence.'

LORD BYRON, poet, *Don Juan*, 1821

'London by night! Rome is poor by comparison.'

GEORGE GISSING, novelist, 1857–1903

'When we arrived in London, my sadness at leaving Paris was turned into despair. After my long stay in the French capital, huge, ponderous, massive London seemed to me as ugly a thing as man could contrive to make … I thought of Paris as a beauty spot on the face of the earth, and of London as a big freckle.'

JAMES WELDON JOHNSON, American author, 1871–1938

'People in London think of London as the centre of the world, whereas New Yorkers think the world ends three miles outside of Manhattan.'

TOBY YOUNG, journalist, b. 1963

'If London is a watercolour, New York is an oil painting.'

SIR PETER SHAFFER, playwright, b. 1926

'Every city has a sex and an age which have nothing to do with demography. Rome is feminine. So is Odessa. London is a teenager, an urchin, and, in this, hasn't changed since the time of Dickens.'

JOHN BERGER, author and critic, 1987

# London Crime

ALTHOUGH IT IS probably no more dangerous than any other city, London is famous for its crooks. From humble Victorian pickpockets to hardened gangsters from the organised-crime empire headed by the Kray twins in the 1960s, London has created more celebrity criminals than any other city – including the most notorious of them all, Jack the Ripper.

If that makes you afraid to go out, remember that London is also home to the world's most famous detective, Sherlock Holmes.

'More than half the memorable murders of Britain have happened in London.'

MARTIN FIDO, author, *The Murder Guide to London*, 1986

'Where the mob gathers, swiftly shoot along,
    Nor idly mingle with the noisy throng.
    Lured by silver hilt, amid the swarm,
    The subtil artist will thy side disarm.
    Nor is thy flaxen wig with safety worn;
    High on the shoulder in a basket born
Lurks the sly boy; whose hand to rapine bred,
    Plucks off the curling honours of thy head.'

JOHN GAY, poet and playwright,
*Trivia, or Walking the Streets of London*, 1716

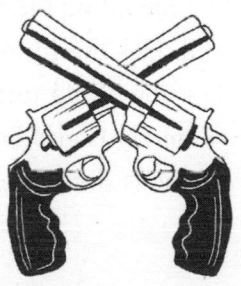

'The day appointed by law for the thief's shame is the day of glory in his own opinion. His procession to Tyburn [London's historic place of execution] and his last moments there are all triumphant, attended with the compassion of the weak and tender-hearted, and with the applause, admiration and envy of all the bold and hardened.'

HENRY FIELDING, novelist and magistrate, *An Enquiry into the Causes of the Late Increase in Robbers*, 1751

'Be quiet, Ings; we can die without all this noise.'

ARTHUR THISTLEWOOD, one of the Cato Street conspirators, at the gallows, annoyed by his co-conspirator's singing, 1820. The Cato Street Conspiracy was a plot to assassinate the British cabinet, including the Prime Minister, in that same year.

'About a twelvemonth ago, as we were strolling through Covent-garden ... we were attracted by the very pre-possessing appearance of a pickpocket, who having declined to take the trouble of walking to the Police-office, on the grounds that he hadn't the slightest wish to go there at all, was being conveyed thither in a wheelbarrow, to the huge delight of a crowd.'

CHARLES DICKENS, novelist, *Sketches by Boz*, 1836

'London! the needy villain's general home,
The common sewer of Paris and of Rome!
With eager thirst, by folly or by fate,
Sucks in the dregs of each corrupted state.'

SAMUEL JOHNSON, writer and polymath, 'London', 1738

'In London all classes are deeply corrupted. Vice comes to them early.'

FLORA TRISTAN, French socialist writer, *London Journal*, 1840

'Dear Boss,

'I keep on hearing the police have caught me, but they won't fix me just yet. I have laughed when they look so clever and talk about me being on the right track. The joke about Leather Apron gave me real fits.

'I am down on whores and I shan't quit ripping them till I do get buckled. Grand work, the last job was. I gave the lady no time to squeal. How can they catch me now? I love my work and want to start again. You will soon hear of me and my funny little games.

'I saved some of the proper red stuff in a ginger beer bottle over the last job, to write with, but it went thick like glue and I can't use it. Red ink is fit enough, I hope. Ha! Ha!

'The next job I do I shall clip the lady's ears off and send them to the police, just for jolly, wouldn't you? Keep this letter back until I do a bit more work, then give it out straight. My knife's so nice and sharp, I want to get to work right away if I get a chance. Good luck,

'Yours truly,

'Jack the Ripper'

Letter received by the CENTRAL NEWS AGENCY,
27 September 1888

'It is my belief, Watson, founded upon my experience, that the lowest and vilest alleys in London do not present a more dreadful record of sin than does the smiling and beautiful countryside.'

SHERLOCK HOLMES, detective, in 'The Adventure of the Copper Beeches' by Sir Arthur Conan Doyle, 1892

'I used to have a list of things from my school buddies of what kind of art material they wanted. I'd go up to the West End of London and spend the whole day knocking stuff off.'

RONALD BIGGS, Great Train Robber, b. 1929

'Unless he is insane, the brown-eyed criminal does not carry a gun with intent to use it. He may think he does but the showdown proves him wrong. The man who shoots to kill has grey eyes.'

SUPERINTENDENT ROBERT FABIAN, Scotland Yard detective, 1901–1978

'Reg Kray's got a lot of nice things about him but he did a lot of things in his life that, if he'd thought about them, he wouldn't have done. He was very much under the influence of his brother who is, without a doubt, a psychopath.'

ERIC MASON, Kray Twins associate, b. 1930

'Ronnie could just sit there and stare at a person for half an hour and that person would go away completely cowed. That was how much fear they generated.'

ALBERT DONOGHUE, Kray Twins associate, b. 1935

'*The Independent* had it wrong when their reporter said I'd been shot dead outside Turnmills nightclub [in Clerkenwell] in 1991. I was only in hospital two days that time.'

'MAD' FRANKIE FRASER, gangland enforcer
and author, *Mad Frank*, 1995

'A good police force is one that catches more criminals than it employs.'

SIR ROBERT MARK, Metropolitan
Police Commissioner, 1972–1977

'When you see a mugging on the Holloway Road, and the villain scarpers into the night, there's no point looking around for a policeman. But in due course the police turn up in a high-powered car, and you are ferried with flashing lights, up and down – in a macho Starsky and Hutch display that has become utterly banal – while the mugger has melted away.'

BORIS JOHNSON, politician,
*Daily Telegraph*, 2000

'The police don't get terribly excited about people who burgle prefabs in Catford, who don't have the ear of the Home Secretary. All my victims were very prestigious people – the only people who end up with vast amounts of money or jewellery are very greedy, predatory people and it's been one of the great privileges of my life to persecute them.'

PETER SCOTT, 'King of the Cat Burglars', b. 1932

'For every person on camera throwing stones there will be a thousand others off camera rebuilding what has been destroyed. This is the Tottenham I was born in, the Tottenham I grew up in and that I live in.'

DAVID LAMMY, London MP, on the summer riots of 2011, 8 August 2011

# London
# Streets

FOR MANY VISITORS to London, the speed and bustle of Londoners going about their business en masse have defined their experience of the city and its people. Denied the calm and hospitality found behind the doors of homes that remain closed to outsiders, the sights and sounds of the streets have fascinated and exhausted them.

For Londoners, the streets are a native element, an endless maze to be explored and enjoyed at leisure.

'The metropolis affords many amusements which are open to all; it is itself an astonishing and perpetual spectacle to the curious eye; and each taste, each sense, may be gratified by the variety of objects that will occur in the long circuit of a morning walk.'

EDWARD GIBBON, historian, 1796

'In the open streetes is such walking, such talking, such running, such riding, such clapping too of windowes, such rapping at Chamber doors, such crying out for drink, such buying up of meate, and such calling uppon Shottes, that at every such time, I verily beleeve I dwell in a Towne of Warre.'

THOMAS DEKKER, dramatist, *c*. 1572–1632

'I wished I could fly for a time to Vienna, to have more quiet in which to work, for the noise that the common people make as they sell their wares in the street is intolerable.'

JOSEPH HAYDN, composer, 1791

'The English walk very fast; their thoughts being entirely engrossed in business, they are very punctual to their appointments, and those, who happen to be in their way, are sure to be sufferers by it; constantly darting forward, they jostle them with a force proportioned to the bulk and velocity of their motion.'

PIERRE-JEAN GROSLEY, French writer, 1772

'Sir, if you wish to have a just notion of the magnitude of this city, you must not be satisfied with seeing its great streets and squares, but must survey the innumerable little lanes and courts. It is not in the showy evolutions of buildings, but in the multiplicity of human habitations which are crowded together, that the wonderful immensity of London consists.'

SAMUEL JOHNSON, writer and polymath, in Boswell's
*Life of Johnson*, 1791

'The streets of London have their map; but our passions are uncharted. What are you going to meet if you turn this corner?'

VIRGINIA WOOLF, novelist, *Jacob's Room*, 1922

'What inexhaustible food for speculation, do the streets of London afford!'

CHARLES DICKENS, novelist, *Sketches by Boz*, 1836

'London is a labyrinth, half of stone and half of flesh. It cannot be conceived in its entirety but can be experienced only as a wilderness of alleys and passages, courts and thoroughfares, in which even the experienced citizen may lose the way.'

PETER ACKROYD, novelist and historian,
*London: The Biography*, 2000

'A town such as London, where a man may wander for hours together without reaching the beginning of the end, is a strange thing.'

FREDERICK ENGELS, German author and philosopher, 1820–1895

'Down in Farringdon Street the carts, wagons, vans, cabs, omnibuses crossed and intermingled in a steaming splash-bath of mud; human beings, reduced to their due paltriness, seemed to toil in exasperation along the strips of pavement, bound on errands, which were a mockery, driven automaton-like by forces they neither understood nor could resist.'

GEORGE GISSING, novelist, *The Nether World*, 1889

'I've been walking about London for the last thirty years, and I find something fresh in it every day.'

SIR WALTER BESANT, historian, 1836–1901

'"I love walking in London," said Mrs Dalloway. "Really, it's better than walking in the country."'

VIRGINIA WOOLF, novelist, *Mrs Dalloway*, 1925

'There is one respect in which a town must be more poetical than the country, since it is closer to the spirit of man; for London, if it be not one of the masterpieces of man, is at least one of his sins. A street is really more poetical than a meadow, because a street has a secret. A street is going somewhere, and a meadow nowhere.'

G K CHESTERTON, author, *The Napoleon of Notting Hill*, 1904

'And that is the strangest thing about English streets: here you do not see respectable ladies telling each other on the kerb what happened at the Smiths or the Greens, nor courting couples strolling arm-in-arm like sleep-walkers, nor worthy citizens seated on their doorstep with their hands on their knees ... nor men drinking in the streets, nor tramps, nor servant-girls, nor pensioners – in short, nothing, nothing, nothing; the London streets are just a gulley through which life flows to get home. In the street people do not live, stare, talk, stand or sit; they merely rush through the streets.'

KAREL ČAPEK, Czech dramatist, 1923

'Proportion … You can't help thinking about it in these London streets, where it doesn't exist … It's like listening to a symphony of cats to walk along them. Senseless discords and a horrible disorder all the way … A concert of Brobdingnagian cats. Order has been turned into a disgusting chaos. We need no barbarians from outside; they're on the premises, all the time.'

ALDOUS HUXLEY, novelist, *Antic Hay*, 1923

'The appearance presented by the streets of London an hour before sunrise, on a summer's morning, is most striking even to the few whose unfortunate pursuits of pleasure, or scarcely less unfortunate pursuits of business, cause them to be well acquainted with the scene.

'There is an air of cold, solitary desolation about the noiseless streets which we are accustomed to see thronged at other times by a busy, eager crowd, and over the quiet, closely-shut buildings, which throughout the day are swarming with life and bustle, that is very impressive.'

CHARLES DICKENS, novelist, *Sketches by Boz*, 1836

'I started noticing how stained the pavements are in London. The pavements in Beverly Hills aren't used; in London, they're used for everything.'

JULIE CHRISTIE, actor, b. 1941

'One thing about London: not so much dogshit everywhere. A lot still. Compared to New York, even old New York, it's the *cloaca maxima*. But nothing like it used to be, when the streets of London were *paved* with dogshit.'

MARTIN AMIS, novelist, *London Fields*, 1989

'When I look at the streets of London I see a future for the planet, a model of cooperation and harmony between races and religions; in which barriers are broken down by tolerance, humour and respect – without giving way either to bigotry, or the petty balkanisation of the Race Relations industry.'

BORIS JOHNSON, politician, *Daily Mail*, 2007

# London Laughs

MOST PEOPLE, EVEN if they have never been in London, have a definite image of it in their heads, and this 'familiarity' has made the city an easy target for comedians and wits for many hundreds of years. However, even the most ardent defender of London would have to admit that, sometimes, they hit the nail on the head.

'The amount of women in London who flirt with their own husbands is perfectly scandalous. It looks so bad. It is simply washing one's clean linen in public.'

OSCAR WILDE, Irish playwright and poet,
*The Importance of Being Earnest*, 1895

'London is a large village on the Thames where the principal industries carried on are music halls and the confidence trick.'

DAN LENO, music hall comedian, 1860–1904

'Respirator, *n.* An apparatus fitted over the nose and mouth of an inhabitant of London, whereby to filter the visible universe in its passage to the lungs.'

AMBROSE BIERCE, American writer and journalist,
*The Devil's Dictionary*, 1911

'I'm leaving because the weather is too good. I hate London when it's not raining.'

GROUCHO MARX, American comedian, 1890–1977

'I meant to sail earlier but waited to finish some studies of what are called Family Hotels. They are a London specialty. God has not permitted them to exist elsewhere. They are ramshackle clubs which were dwellings at the time of the Heptarchy. Dover and Albemarle Streets are filled with them.

'The once spacious rooms are split up into coops which afford as much discomfort as can be had anywhere out of jail for any money. All the modern inconveniences are furnished, and some that have been obsolete for a century. The prices are astonishingly high for what you get ...

'The rooms are as interesting as the Tower of London, but older I think. Older and dearer. The lift was a gift of William the Conqueror. Some of the beds are prehistoric. They represent geological periods.'

MARK TWAIN, author and journalist, letter to
J Y M MacAlister, September 1900, from
*Selected Letters of Mark Twain*, published 1982

'When it's three o'clock in New York, it's still 1938 in London.'

BETTE MIDLER, comedian and actor, b. 1945

'In London they don't like you if you're still alive.'

HARVEY FIERSTEIN, American playwright and actor, b. 1952

'My cousin's gay; he went to London only to find out that Big Ben was a clock.'

RODNEY DANGERFIELD,
American comedian, 1921–2004

'London is full of women who trust their husbands. One can always recognise them. They look so thoroughly unhappy.'

OSCAR WILDE, Irish playwright and poet,
*Lady Windemere's Fan*, 1892

'London – a place you go to get bronchitis.'

FRAN LEBOWITZ, American author, b. 1950

'I don't know what London's coming to – the higher the buildings the lower the morals.'

NOËL COWARD, playwright and actor, 1899–1973

'The man who is tired of London is tired of looking for a parking space.'

PAUL THEROUX, American novelist, 1998

'London Transport commissioned a study to find out why buses were running late and it turned out it was because they kept stopping to let people on.'

RORY MCGRATH, comedian, b. 1956

'Go to London. I guarantee you'll either be mugged or not appreciated. Catch the train to London, stopping at Rejection, Disappointment, Backstabbing Central and Shattered Dreams Parkway.'

ALAN PARTRIDGE, television personality, *I'm Alan Partridge*, series 2, episode 2, 2002

# London
# Suburbs

ALTHOUGH THE HISTORIC centre of London dominates our concept of the city, for most Londoners their everyday experience of the city happens five or ten miles distant from Westminster and the City, in the vast hinterland of London's suburbs.

'An acre in Middlesex is better than a principality in Utopia.'

THOMAS BABINGTON MACAULAY, politician and historian, 1843

'Go down to Kew in lilac-time, in lilac-time, in lilac-time, Go down to Kew in lilac-time (it isn't far from London!).'

ALFRED NOYES, poet, 'The Barrel-Organ', 1904

'I cannot think why people should think the names of places in the country more poetical than those in London. Shallow romanticists go away in trains and stop in places called Hugmy-in-the-Hole, or Bumps-on-the-Puddle. And all the time they could, if they liked, go and live at a place with the dim, divine name of St John's Wood.

'I have never been to St John's Wood. I dare not. I should be afraid of the innumerable night of fir trees, afraid to come upon a blood-red cup and the beating wings of the eagle. But all these things can be imagined by remaining reverently in the Harrow train.'

G K CHESTERTON, author, *The Napoleon of Notting Hill*, 1904

'The suburbs of London have a peculiar charm; between the little houses and gardens there are open spots covered with grass and generally with a church or school or workhouse in the middle among the trees and shrubs. It can be so beautiful there when the sun is setting red in the thin evening mist.'

VINCENT VAN GOGH, artist, in a letter to his brother Theo, 7 October 1876, from *Complete Letters of Vincent Van Gogh*, published 1958

'The huge peaceful wilderness of outer London, the barges on the miry river, the familiar streets, the posters telling of cricket matches and Royal weddings, the men in bowler hats, the pigeons in Trafalgar Square, the red buses, the blue policemen – all sleeping the deep, deep sleep of England.'

GEORGE ORWELL, writer, *Homage to Catalonia*, 1938

'There are some parts of London which are necessary and others which are contingent. Everywhere west of Earls Court is contingent, except for a few places along the river.'

IRIS MURDOCH, novelist, *Under the Net*, 1954

# Lonely London

ALL PLACES CAN be lonely for strangers, but the overwhelming scale of London, the dour streets and the dispassionate inhabitants who silently pass in them, have long been the cause of alienation and melancholy for those used to more friendly berths.

'Melancholy prevails in London in every family, in circles, in assemblies, at public and private entertainments … The merry meetings, even of the lowest sort, are dashed with this gloom.'

PIERRE-JEAN GROSLEY, French writer, 1772

'For miles before you reach a suburb of London such as Islington, for instance, a last great sign and augury of the immensity which belongs to the coming metropolis forces itself upon the dullest observer, in the growing sense of his own utter insignificance.

'Everywhere else in England, you yourself, horses, carriage, attendants (if you travel with any) are regarded with attention, perhaps even curiosity; at all events, you are seen. But after passing the final posthouse on every avenue to London, for the latter ten or twelve miles, you become aware that you are no longer noticed: nobody sees you; nobody hears you; nobody regards you; you do not even regard yourself.'

THOMAS DE QUINCEY, *Autobiographical Sketches*, 1853

'London is as complete a solitude as the plains of Syria.'

CHARLES DICKENS, novelist, *Nicholas Nickleby*, 1839

'This melancholy London – I sometimes imagine that the souls of the lost are compelled to walk through its streets perpetually. One feels them passing like a whiff of air.'

W B YEATS, Irish poet, letter to Katharine Tynan, 25 August 1888

'When I married Paul, we lived in St John's Wood in London. We had nice next-door neighbours, but you don't know anyone else. Everyone lives in isolation.'

LINDA MCCARTNEY, photographer and musician, 1941–1998

'The brutal indifference, the unfeeling isolation of each … is nowhere so shamelessly bare-fared … as just here in the crowding of the great city.'

FRIEDRICH ENGELS, German author and philosopher, 1820–1895

'The early clerk population of Somers and Camden towns, Islington, and Pentonville, are fast pouring into the city, or directing their steps towards Chancery-lane and the Inns of Court. Middle-aged men, whose salaries have by no means increased in the same proportion as their families, plod steadily along, apparently with no object in view but the counting-house; knowing by sight almost everybody they meet or overtake, for they have seen them every morning (Sunday excepted) during the last twenty years, but speaking to no one. If they do happen to overtake a personal acquaintance, they just exchange a hurried salutation, and keep walking on either by his side, or in front of him, as his rate of walking may chance to be. As to stopping to shake hands, or to take the friend's arm, they seem to think that as it is not included in their salary, they have no right to do it.'

CHARLES DICKENS, novelist, *Sketches by Boz*, 1836

'No man ever was left to himself for the first time in the streets, as yet unknown, of London, but he must have been saddened and mortified, perhaps terrified, by the sense of desertion and utter loneliness which belongs to his situation.'

THOMAS DE QUINCEY, writer, *Autobiographical Sketches*, 1853

'I reached London and stayed in a hotel. Everyone seemed like phantoms. The hotel used to empty after breakfast and I watched the crowded streets. I was in despair. It was not possible to know this humanity or enter into the heart of another place.'

RABINDRANATH TAGORE, Indian poet, 1912

'There is no town in the world which is more adapted for training one away from people and training one into solitude than London. The manner of life, the distances, the climate, the very multitude of the population in which personality vanishes, all this together with the absence of Continental diversions conduces to the same effect.'

ALEXANDER HERZEN, Russian intellectual, 1885

'At the historic centre there is nothing but a civic void, which fills and empties daily with armies of clerks and dealers, mostly citizens of other towns. The true identity of London, he said, is in its absence. As a city it no longer exists. In this alone it is truly modern. London was the first metropolis to disappear.'

PATRICK KEILLER, film-maker and writer, *London*, 1994

'It is strange with how little notice, good, bad, or indifferent, a man may live and die in London. He awakens no sympathy in the breast of any single person; his existence is a matter of interest to no one save himself; he cannot be said to be forgotten when he dies, for no one remembered him when he was alive.'

CHARLES DICKENS, novelist, *Sketches by Boz*, 1836

# London
# Nights

IN MEDIEVAL LONDON it was forbidden to be outside after dark, but in later centuries, London's reputation as a twenty-four-hour city began to grow. The advent of gaslight lent the night an enchanting poetry and brilliance. It was never a place of absolute quiet or safety, but for many writers the nocturnal streets revealed the city's true face.

'It was a dark and stormy night; the rain fell in torrents – except at occasional intervals, when it was checked by a violent gust of wind which swept up the streets (for it is in London that our scene lies), rattling along the housetops, and fiercely agitating the scanty flame of the lamps that struggled against the darkness.'

EDWARD G BULWER-LYTTON, politician and novelist, with the legendary opening sentence of *Paul Clifford*, 1830

'But the streets of London, to be beheld in the very height of their glory, should be seen on a dark, dull, murky winter's night, when there is just enough damp gently stealing down to make the pavement greasy, without cleansing it of any of its impurities; and when the heavy lazy mist, which hangs over every object, makes the gas-lamps look brighter, and the brilliantly-lighted shops more splendid, from the contrast they present to the darkness around.'

CHARLES DICKENS, novelist, *Sketches by Boz*, 1836

'Such a glare is cast by the gaslights, I knew not where I was after sunset.'

HESTER THRALE, diarist, 1817

'In the evening I strolled out, and walked as far as St Paul's – never getting enough of the bustle of London, which may weary, but can never satisfy me. By night London looks wild and dreamy, and fills me with a sort of pleasant dread.'

NATHANIEL HAWTHORNE, American novelist,
*English Notebooks*, 1853

'At night, this is a strange part of town. It takes a while to realise why, but then it'll hit you: the roads might be busy with traffic, but no one is walking around. *No one*. People who live in Knightsbridge don't walk because they don't need to walk.'

*Time Out Guide to London*, 2003

'London was beginning to illuminate herself against the night. Electric lights sizzled and jagged in the main thoroughfares, gas lamps in the side-streets glimmered a canary gold or green. The sky was a crimson battlefield of spring, but London was not afraid.'

E M FORSTER, novelist, *Howard's End*, 1910

'London is so beautiful in summer. It lay beneath my window, a fairy city veiled in golden mist, for I worked in a room high above the chimney-pots; and at night the lights shone far beneath me, so that I looked down as into an Aladdin's cave of jewels.'

JEROME K JEROME, novelist, 1859–1927

'When the evening mist clothes the riverside with poetry, as with a veil, and the poor buildings lose themselves in the dim sky, and the tall chimneys become campanili, and the warehouses are palaces in the night, and the whole city hangs in the heavens, and fairy-land is before us – then the wayfarer hastens home; the working man and the cultured one, the wise man and the one of pleasure, cease to understand, as they have ceased to see, and Nature, who, for once, has sung in tune, sings her exquisite song to the artist alone.'

JAMES MCNEILL WHISTLER, artist, 1890

'Someday when peace has returned to this odd world I want to come to London again and stand on a certain balcony on a moonlit night and look down upon the peaceful silver curve of the Thames with its dark bridges.'

ERNIE PYLE, American war correspondent, 1900–1945

'I have not observed that London ever goes to bed.'

NATHANIEL HAWTHORNE, American novelist,
*English Notebooks*, 1853

# London
# Weather

FIFTY YEARS AFTER the Clean Air Act 1956 removed the fog and smog of old London forever, the Victorian image of mist-shrouded courtyards still dominates the imagination of many visitors. The following quotes do not hide the extent to which fog did once typify London's weather, but also serve to reassure us that the occasional glorious spring day is to be expected.

'All the forces which have produced the London sky have made something which all Londoners know, and which no one who has never seen London has ever seen.'

G K CHESTERTON, writer, 1874–1936

'Yesterday, having some tickets to the Zoological Gardens, we went thither with the two eldest children. It was a most beautiful sunny day, the very perfection of English weather – which is as much as to say, the best weather in the world.'

NATHANIEL HAWTHORNE, American novelist,
*English Notebooks*, 1853

'This is a London particular … A fog, miss.'

CHARLES DICKENS, novelist, *Bleak House*, 1853

'Victorian fog is the world's most famous meteorological phenomenon.'

PETER ACKROYD, novelist and historian,
*London: The Biography*, 2000

'It was a foggy day in London, and the fog was heavy and dark. Animate London, with smarting eyes and irritated lungs, was blinking, wheezing, and choking; inanimate London was a sooty spectre, divided in purpose between being visible and invisible, and so being wholly neither.'

CHARLES DICKENS, novelist, *Our Mutual Friend*, 1865

'This fog seems an atmosphere proper to huge, grimy London ... The fog was denser than ever, very black indeed, more like a distillation of mud than anything else; the ghost of mud, the spiritualised medium of departed mud, through which the departed citizens of London probably tread in the Hades whither they are translated. So heavy was the gloom, that gas was lighted in all the shop windows; and the little charcoal furnaces of the women and boys roasting chestnuts threw a ruddy misty glow around them.'

NATHANIEL HAWTHORNE, American novelist,
*English Notebooks*, 1855

'I think very often under these radiant skies of the London fogs and always regretfully. Individually speaking I was evidently intended to be an Englishman.'

GIUSEPPE MAZZINI, Italian patriot, 1849

'Fog everywhere. Fog up the river, where it flows among green aits and meadows; fog down the river, where it rolls defiled among the tiers of shipping and the waterside pollutions of a great (and dirty) city. Fog on the Essex marshes, fog on the Kentish heights. Fog creeping into the cabooses of collier-brigs; fog lying out on the yards, and hovering in the rigging of great ships; fog drooping on the gunwales of barges and small boats. Fog in the eyes and throats of ancient Greenwich pensioners, wheezing by the firesides of their wards; fog in the stem and bowl of the afternoon pipe of the wrathful skipper, down in his close cabin; fog cruelly pinching the toes and fingers of his shivering little 'prentice boy on deck. Chance people on the bridges peeping over the parapets into a nether sky of fog, with fog all round them, as if they were up in a balloon, and hanging in the misty clouds.'

CHARLES DICKENS, novelist, *Bleak House*, 1853

'I love this perpetually grey sky. You don't need to think. The bright blue sky and the stars are really frightening things. You can feel at home here, and God cannot see you. His spy, the sun, does not care to come out of his shadows.'

STÉPHANE MALLARMÉ, French poet, 1863

'It was a Sunday afternoon, wet and cheerless; and a duller spectacle this earth of ours has not to show than a rainy Sunday in London.'

THOMAS DE QUINCEY, writer,
*Confessions of an English Opium-Eater*, 1821

'What an amazing thing is the coming of spring to London. The very pavements seem ready to crack and lift under the denied earth; in the air is a consciousness of life which tells you that if traffic stopped for a fortnight grass would grow again in Piccadilly and corn would spring in pavement cracks where a horse had spilt his "feed". And the squares of London, so dingy and black since the first

October gale, fill week by week with the rising tide of life, just as the sea, running up the creeks and pushing itself forward inch by inch towards the land, comes at last to each remote rock pool.'

H V MORTON, journalist, *In Search of England*, 1927

# Creative London

LONDON HAS BEEN home to thousands of artists, writers, painters and poets, as well as countless actors, scientists and creative people from every field. Some have taken inspiration from the city itself, while for others it has been the ideal place to work. Others still have had their creative flame snuffed out by the city's oppressive, competitive atmosphere.

'So poetry, which is in Oxford made
An art, in London is only a trade.'

JOHN DRYDEN, poet, 'Prologue to the University of Oxford', 1673

'Johnson now thought of trying his fortune in London, the great field of genius and exertion, where talents of every kind have the fullest scope, and the highest encouragement.'

JAMES BOSWELL, writer, *Life of Johnson*, 1791

'I must have a London audience. I could never preach, but to the educated; to those who were capable of estimating my composition.'

JANE AUSTEN, novelist, *Mansfield Park*, 1814

'Do not send a poet to London. The bleak seriousness of everything, the colossal uniformity, the machine-like movement, the peevishness even of joy – this over-driven London oppresses the fancy and tears the heart.'

HEINRICH HEINE, German poet, 1827

'In London, the weather would affect me negatively. I react strongly to light. If it is cloudy and raining, there are clouds and rain in my soul.'

JERZY KOSINSKI, Polish-American novelist, 1933–1991

'Up to this time I have been crushed under a sense of the sheer magnitude of London – its inconceivable immensity – in such a way as to paralyse my mind. The place sits on you, broods on you, stamps on you.'

HENRY JAMES, novelist, 1869

'Educated girls have a pronounced distaste for London garrets; not one in fifty thousand would share poverty with the brightest genius ever born.'

GEORGE GISSING, novelist, *New Grub Street*, 1891

'An actor who knows his business ought to be able to make the London telephone directory sound enthralling.'

SIR DONALD SINDEN, actor, b. 1923

'I came to London. It had become the centre of my world and I had worked hard to come to it. And I was lost.'

V S NAIPAUL, writer, *An Area of Darkness*, 1964

'I wonder how many young men fall utterly to pieces from being turned loose into London.'

ANTHONY TROLLOPE, novelist, 1815–1882

'I went to London because, for me, it was the home of literature. I went there because of Dickens and Shakespeare.'

BEN OKRI, Nigerian novelist, b. 1959

'Because I was conscious of brains, I thought that the only place for me was London. It's easy enough to understand this common delusion. We form our ideas of London from old literature; we think of London as if it were still the one centre of intellectual life; we think and talk like Chatterton. But the truth is that intellectual men in our day do their best to keep away from London ...

'It's a huge misfortune, this will-o'-the-wisp attraction exercised by London on young men of brains. They come here to be degraded, or to perish, when their true sphere is a life of peaceful remoteness. The type of man capable of success in London is more or less callous and cynical. If I had the training of boys, I would teach them to think of London as the last place where life can be lived worthily.'

GEORGE GISSING, novelist, *New Grub Street*, 1891

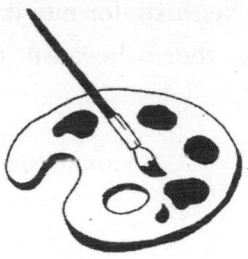

'Whenever I want to get an idea for painting or writing, I always throw myself among the thickest crowds such as Earls Court or Shepherd's Bush.'

YOSHIO MARKINO, Japanese artist, 1869–1956

'It is a sorrowful but I fear too certain truth that no place is at all equal, for aiding one in Natural History pursuits, to this dirty smoky town.'

CHARLES DARWIN, naturalist, in a letter to the Revd W D Fox, 12 March 1837

'The best bribe which London offers today to the imagination is that, in such a vast variety of people and conditions, one can believe there is room for persons of romantic character to exist, and that the poet, the mystic, and the hero may hope to confront their counterparts.'

RALPH WALDO EMERSON, American poet, 1860

'Samuel Johnson: The happiness of London is not to be conceived but by those who have been in it. I will venture to say, there is more learning and science within the circumference of ten miles from where we now sit, than in all the rest of the world.

'James Boswell: The only disadvantage is the great distance at which people live from one another.

'Johnson: Yes, Sir, but that is occasioned by the largeness of it, which is the cause of all the other advantages.'

From JAMES BOSWELL's *Life of Johnson*, 1791

# London
# Celebrated

LONDON HAS SOMETIMES created in its most ardent fans a peculiar chauvinism whereby nowhere better or more worthy is imaginable. We might not always share their enthusiasm for the city's every aspect, but the passion can be inspiring nonetheless.

'London, thou art of townes A *per se.*
Soveraign of cities, semeliest in sight,
Of high renoun, riches, and royaltie;
Of lordis, barons, and many goodly knyght;
Of most delectable lusty ladies bright;
Of famous prelatis in hobitis clericall;
Of merchauntis full of substance and myght:
London, thou art the flour of Cities all.'

WILLIAM DUNBAR, poet, 'To the City of London', *c.* 1500

'After the music of the words "London only" at Reading, we gave ourselves up to the *nil admirari* spirit. The size and importance of the terminus might alarm a timid fellow passenger, but were nothing to us. The wet streets … the reflections from the street lamps and the shops, the utter indifference of everybody to us and our concerns – why was it fascinating even to a child? I suppose we took on that feeling of superiority to all the world, the idea of finality, that London gives. No signposts to other towns are to be seen. Here's London. Here you are.'

M V HUGHES, author, *A London Child of the Seventies*, 1934

'London is the capital of all capitals.'

STEEN EILER RASMUSSEN, writer and architect, 1937

'The marvellous maturity of London! I would rather be dead in this town than preening my feathers in heaven.'

NICHOLAS MONSARRAT, novelist, 1910–1979

'Oh, I love this city! I love it. Wherever I go in the world, to land back in London is the best feeling. I get to see so many amazing places when I'm working, like Miami, and I think, "I could live here." But then I go, "Yeah, but I wouldn't be in London."'

AMY WINEHOUSE, musician, 2007

'It is utterly true that he who cannot find wonder, mystery, awe, the sense of a new world and an undiscovered realm in the places by the Grays Inn Road will never find those secrets elsewhere, not in the heart of Africa.'

ARTHUR MACHEN, author and mystic, 1863–1947

# London Cursed

JUST AS IT embodies for some all imaginable virtues, London has as often represented the ultimate horror of existence, a vast and pitiless mechanism for degrading humanity. The anguished quotes that follow are unlikely to feature in the tourist brochures.

'I do not at all like that city. All sorts of men crowd together there from every country under the heavens. Each race brings its own vices and its own customs to the city. No one lives in it without falling into some sort of crime. Every quarter of it abounds in great obscenities …Whatever evil or malicious thing that can be found in any part of the world, you will find in that one city.

'Do not associate with the crowds of pimps; do not mingle with the throngs in the eating-houses; avoid the dice and gambling, the theatre and the tavern. You will meet with more braggarts there than in all France; the number of parasites is infinite … jesters, smooth-skinned lads, Moors, flatterers, pretty boys, effeminates, pederasts, singing and dancing girls, quacks, belly-dancers, sorceresses, extortioners, night-wanderers, magicians, mimes, beggars, buffoons: all this tribe fill all the houses. Therefore, if you do not want to dwell with evil-doers, do not live in London.'

RICHARD OF DEVIZES, monk, *c.* 1190

'London is a place which I remember with a haunting horror, as if I had been confined there.'

KEIR HARDIE, politician, 1901

'Long ago it was discovered that London devours her own children.'

SIR WALTER BESANT, historian, 1836–1901

'The capital is become an overgrown monster; which, like a dropsical head, will in time leave the body and extremities without nourishment and support.'

TOBIAS SMOLLETT, novelist,
*The Expedition of Humphry Clinker*, 1771

'As sure as the devil is in London.'

Traditional saying, eighteenth century

'Hell is a city much like London –
A populous and a smoky city;
There are all sorts of people undone,
And there is little or no fun done;
Small justice shown, and still less pity.'

PERCY BYSSHE SHELLEY, poet, 'Peter Bell the Third', 1839

'In London you no longer see the populace. Instead, you see a loss of sensibility, systematic, resigned, and encouraged.'

FYODOR DOSTOEVSKY, Russian novelist, 1863

'I walk to Oxford Street and climb on the number 8. It's freezing and it starts to rain and it's the ugliest bus I've ever seen, rattling down the ugliest streets, in the ugliest city, in the ugliest country, in the ugliest of all possible worlds.'

DAVID THEWLIS, actor and novelist, The Late Hector Kipling, 2007

'If the street life, not the Whitechapel street life, but that of the common but so-called respectable part of town is in any city more gloomy, more ugly, more grimy, more cruel than in London, I certainly don't care to see it. Sometimes it occurs to one that possibly all the failures of this generation, the world over, have been suddenly swept into London, for the streets are a restless, breathing, malodorous pageant of the seedy of all nations.'

WILLA CATHER, American novelist, 1902

'And the first half-hour in London, after some years abroad, is really a plunge of misery. The strange, the grey and uncanny, almost deathly sense of *dullness* is overwhelming. Of course you get over it after a while, and admit that you exaggerated. You get into the rhythm of London again, and you tell yourself that it is *not* dull. And yet you are haunted, all the time, sleeping or waking, with the uneasy feeling: It is dull! It is all dull! This life here is one vast complex of dullness! I am dull. I am being dulled. My spirit is being dulled! My life is dulling down to London dullness.'

D H LAWRENCE, novelist,
'Why I Don't Like Living in London', 1928

'I believe we shall come to care about people less and less, Helen. The more people one knows, the easier it becomes to replace them. It's one of the curses of London.'

E M FORSTER, novelist, *Howards End*, 1910

# Historic London

LONDON HAS EXISTED for almost two thousand years, and writers have often been moved to think on the meaning of the city's endurance after feeling the weight of its history on their shoulders. Others have looked forward to that inevitable day when the great city of London is no more.

'What's not destroyed by Time's devouring hand?
Where's Troy, and where's the Maypole in the Strand?'

JAMES BRAMSTON, poet, *The Art of Politics*, 1729

'Nor perhaps is there a single spot in London in which the past is not visibly present to us, either in the shape of some old buildings or at least in the names of the streets.'

LEIGH HUNT, writer, 1848

'He describes London like a special correspondent for posterity.'

WALTER BAGEHOT, essayist, on Charles Dickens, 1858

'The narrowest street possesses, in every crook and twist of its intention, the soul of the man who built it, perhaps long in his grave. Every brick has as human a hieroglyph as if it were a graven brick of Babylon: every slate on the roof is as educational a document as if it were a slate covered with addition and subtraction sums.'

G K CHESTERTON, writer, 1874–1936

'London has the strange effect of making one feel personally historic.'

V S PRITCHETT, author, *London Perceived*, 1962

'The next Augustan Age will dawn on the other side of the Atlantic. There will, perhaps, be a Thucydides at Boston, a Xenophon at New York, and, in time, a Virgil at Mexico, and a Newton at Peru. At last, some curious traveller from Lima will visit England and give a description of the ruins of St Paul's.'

HORACE WALPOLE, writer, 1774

# Author's Note on Sources

Where precise sources and dates of quotations are known, they have been given in full. Otherwise, the dates of birth and death of the person quoted have been used, to indicate the era from which the quote originates.

For quotes from novels and plays, the author name is cited, unless the name of the character is especially significant.

The majority of contributors are of British origin, but the nationality of less well-known foreign contributors has been mentioned wherever it was needed for clarity.

Every reasonable effort has been made to contact copyright holders of material reproduced in this book. If any have inadvertently been overlooked, the publishers would be glad to hear from them and make good in future editions any errors or omissions brought to their attention.

J B EDWARDS

# Select Bibliography

Many of the sources I drew upon in compiling *The Wit & Wisdom of London* are already credited within the book itself. However, the following were also of particular help:

Bailey, Paul (ed.), *The Oxford Book of London*, 1995

Campbell, Duncan, *The Underworld*, 1994

Dale, Iain, *The Bigger Book of Boris*, 2011

Engels, Frederick, *The Condition of the Working-Class in England in 1844*, 1844

Knowles, Elizabeth (ed.), *The Oxford Dictionary of Quotations*, 2009

Rennison, Nick, *The London Blue Plaque Guide*, 1999

Weinreb, Ben and Hibbert, Christopher (ed.), *The London Encyclopedia*, 1993

Wilson, A N (ed.), *The Faber Book of London*, 1993

Wilson, Francesca M, *Strange Island*, 1955

# Acknowledgements

Pages 10, 48, 65, 73, 77, 104, 141 and 167.   Quotations from *London: A Biography* by Peter Ackroyd, published by Chatto & Windus. Reprinted by permission of The Random House Group Limited.

Page 15.   With thanks to David Higham Associates as the representatives of the Estate of Henry Howarth Bashford.

Pages 32 and 33.   Reproduced with permission of Curtis Brown, London on behalf of the Estate of Sir Winston Churchill. Copyright © Winston S. Churchill.

Page 44. *Harry Potter and the Philosopher's Stone* – Copyright © J K Rowling 1997.

Pages 59, 63, 64, 92, 103 and 189.   Extracts from *London Perceived* and *A Cab at the Door* and all other V S Pritchett quotations by V S Pritchett reprinted by permission of Peters Fraser & Dunlop (www.petersfraserdunlop.com) on behalf of the Estate of V S Pritchett.

Page 66.   From 'The London Breed' by Benjamin Zephaniah, *Too Black, Too Strong* (Bloodaxe Books, 2001).

Pages 74, 76 and 84.   With acknowledgement to the Society of Authors as the Literary Representative of the Estate of George Bernard Shaw.

Pages 88–9 and 185.   Published with the permission of the Willa Cather Literary Trust.

Page 153.   With acknowledgement to the Society of Authors as the Literary Representative of the Estate of Alfred Noyes.